The
KITCHEN
ASSISTANT

The
KITCHEN
ASSISTANT

*Time and Money Saving Tips
in the Kitchen*

DARLA P. JAROS

TATE PUBLISHING *& Enterprises*

The Kitchen Assistant
Copyright © 2009 by Darla P. Jaros. All rights reserved.

The opinions expressed by the author are not necessarily those of Tate Publishing, LLC.

Published by Tate Publishing & Enterprises, LLC
127 E. Trade Center Terrace | Mustang, Oklahoma 73064 USA
1.888.361.9473 | www.tatepublishing.com

Tate Publishing is committed to excellence in the publishing industry. The company reflects the philosophy established by the founders, based on Psalm 68:11,
"The Lord gave the word and great was the company of those who published it."

Book design copyright © 2009 by Tate Publishing, LLC. All rights reserved.
Cover design by Lance Waldrop
Interior design by Lindsay B. Behrens

Published in the United States of America

ISBN: 978-1-60799-248-6
1. Cooking / Methods / Quick & Easy   2. Cooking / Entertaining
09.11.03

If you have a kitchen tip, recipe, or a kitchen idea you would like to share for the next edition or have any kitchen related questions, email the information or questions to thekitchenassistant@yahoo.com or send information to:

The Kitchen Assistant, 2596 Desmond Rd., Waterford, MI, 48329.

DEDICATION

This book is dedicated to my beautiful children, Andrea, Anthony, and Alicia. Thanks for being such good kids during our tough times and making my life as a single mom fun. You've kept my life full of love, laughter, and lots of drama, and I feel truly blessed for the experience. I love you all more than words can describe.

Mom

TABLE OF CONTENTS

FOREWORD

Thinking back to meal times as a growing adolescent is such a pleasant memory. With two siblings and a busy, hard–working single mother, the one thing that kept us close was my mother's ability to whip up a good meal. Although money was tight, she always managed to create something special with what seemed like nothing. These family meal times are what helped create our strong family bond. I am truly proud that my mother continues to follow her dreams as she becomes an author who shares her wisdom and techniques with the world. I believe that her recipes and ideas will inspire those who read this first edition and those that follow for many years come.

Alicia Jaros

INTRODUCTION

I fell in love with cooking in my first home economics class when I was fifteen. It was apple season in Michigan, and a couple of the first recipes we made in class were apple crepes and fried apple fritters. They were tasty and easy to make, and I was so impressed with these recipes, I wrote their contents down on the inside cover of an old cookbook my mom had given me.

I excelled at cooking, and during my two years of home economics classes in high school, I took a lot of notes and either wrote them on the blank pages of my old cookbook or on pieces of paper and shoved them between its pages. I've been collecting recipes and helpful kitchen tips for over thirty years and storing them in that book. My poor cookbook became so jammed with all the extra paper that the binders have fallen off, a few pages have come unglued, and I've been using rubber bands to hold it all together. I decided that if I wanted to pass any of this information on to my family and save what's left of my cookbook, I should organize all my notes. This is how this book began.

My old cookbook is still held together with rubber bands, but thankfully it's much thinner these days. The contents of this book now contain a good many of my kitchen tips, a few recipes, as well as other good information to know about your kitchen including various food items that have multiple uses, spices and how to use them, how to cook fish, and my own weight management guide.

Much of this information was born out of necessity to help me maximize my efforts in the kitchen. I needed to save time and money during tight and hectic financial times raising three youngsters without support, and food was my biggest expense. Toilet paper was the second biggest expense, but that's another story all by itself. Needless to say, my cookbook and notes have served me well throughout the years, and I feel blessed to now share them, as well as my thoughts and techniques, with my family and friends.

The weight loss section was born out of my desire to manage my own weight after I quit smoking. It's logical information about weight loss and weight management that's based on a simple math formula that I developed and use to manage my own weight without having to pay someone for help. It's a simple principle that works. I believe in logic, simplicity, and, of course, saving money.

Although my children are now grown, I'm still making my meals from scratch to save a dime and time in the kitchen. I've also become the queen of one–pan, tasty meals that require very little clean up. This frees up more quality time to spend with my grown children and their families when they visit. I'll include more of these meals and techniques in the next edition of this book.

Finally, I've discovered that the kitchen is the one room in the house that can be the most stressful and expensive if you're uninformed. I hope some of this information can help alleviate some of that stress and possibly assist another on how to navigate his or her own kitchen through tough, lean times. Just remember to schedule some fun time during those rough times with your children and enjoy them while they are young. Check out the "Playtime & Crafts" section of the "Make Your Own" chapter for a few kid–friendly, family–oriented projects that are easy to make, easy on the pocketbook or wallet, and fun too!

May the good Lord bless you and yours as he has blessed me and mine.

A SHOESTRING BUDGET
AND PRAYER

I honed my cooking talents in the 1980s while raising three children under the age of five as a single mom. Thanks to those lean days, lots of prayer, and a Polish grandmother who never threw anything away, I learned how to stretch a dollar and literally make a meal out of seemingly nothing in my kitchen.

The only complaint my kids had during our welfare days was when I added powdered milk and water to a half gallon of whole milk to make it look like a full gallon of whole milk. They noticed the difference in taste immediately and it didn't go over well. And although I did that only once, they've never let me forget it.

I never tried to stretch the milk again, but I did discover an infinite number of ways to use those little cans of buttermilk biscuits to make a meal or a dessert. My family preferred the buttermilk flavor and they were, and still are, cheap. I could make a dinner, snack, or dessert out of them and they were the perfect size for little appetites.

To make a dinner out of them, I'd roll a biscuit out flat and wrap them around a hotdog and bake them in a non–greased pan at 325 degrees until the biscuit puffed and lightly browned. Or I'd roll two biscuits out flat, place a cooked hamburger patty, sausage patty, ham, chicken, bacon, or a cooked egg with cheese on one half, place the other flat biscuit on top, crimp the edges together with a fork and bake at 325 degrees until golden brown. Don't worry if you don't have a rolling pin, as a clean jar or can lightly dusted with flour will do. These biscuits also make great mini pizzas as well. Simply flatten them out, spread a little tomato sauce on them, add your favorite toppings, including cheese, and bake at 325 degrees until they brown.

To make a dessert out of these biscuits for my children, I'd use the cap from a milk gallon to cut a hole in each biscuit to make them into donuts. I'd then lightly fry the donut ring and hole in hot oil until golden brown, removed to a paper towel to drain excess oil, and dust with powdered sugar and/or cinnamon sugar. It was always my children's job to dust them with the sugars after I pulled them out of the hot oil. This is a treat they now make for their families.

Another dessert I made with these cheap, little biscuits was a raisin or chocolate chip pull–a–part cake. I'd use two packages of biscuits and cut each single one into four pieces and drop into a bowl. I'd then melt a stick of butter and pour it over the biscuit pieces. I'd add to this mixture about half a cup of sugar (white or brown), a teaspoon of cinnamon, a cup of raisins, chocolate chips, left over Halloween chocolates (chopped, whatever was available) and stir lightly to coat the biscuits. I'd then pour the mixture into a loaf, Bundt, or cake pan and bake at about 325–350 degrees until the biscuits were done. A cake tester or toothpick inserted into the center should come out clean. The uses for these little biscuits are endless and can certainly help stretch a meal when you're on a budget.

I also discovered that if I had certain staple items that had a reasonable shelf life hanging around the kitchen, I could make a decent meal for my family, even when it seemed like the cupboards and refrigerator were empty. Staples are kitchen foods that generally do not need refrigeration and have a relatively long shelf life. Even though staple items generally do not need refrigeration, I keep a good many of my mine in a crisper drawer in the refrigerator to keep the bugs and moths from nesting in them during warmer weather. I've included a list of staple items that I always keep handy in my kitchen, along with a few recipes that utilize these staple foods to help stretch your grocery dollars.

Serving a piece of homemade bread, be it carrot bread or blueberry banana bread, instead of regular toasted bread with breakfast cereals before school or as an after–school snack is a healthier choice for you and your family. These breads can be prepared ahead and frozen to save time and money in the kitchen too. I've included a few of my family's favorite recipes that I hope you enjoy as much as we do.

Making anything from scratch takes a little more time, but the flavor of the end result is well worth the effort. Having your children help with meal preparations will get the job done quicker. It also encourages them to eat what they helped prepare. But the best reward of having your children help out in the kitchen is that one day they will not only cook for themselves, but you too. Just remember to make your mealtime a fun time, especially during the down–and–out times.

RECIPES OR NOTES

STAPLES TO KEEP ON HAND IN THE KITCHEN

Staples are goods that need no refrigeration and have an extended shelf life. As long as you have a few of these items in your kitchen, making a "something out of nothing" meal for your family is possible. Keep cooking oils and shortening tightly closed in the refrigerator to help them maintain their fresh flavor and extend their shelf life (See **Kitchen Tip #146**).

The following are items to include on your grocery list to help you make a meal for your family with just a few basic ingredients when you're on a limited budget. With these staples handy in your kitchen, the next few pages of recipes, ideas, and helpful tips will show you how to make a healthy, tasty meal for your family—even when you think the cupboards are bare. You'll also learn how to make your own pizza, gnocchi, pierogies, flavored vinegars, oils, play dough for the kids, and more. These are just some of the recipes I've used through the years to help stretch my grocery dollars and still turn out a satisfying meal for my family while having a little fun in the process. Be sure to pay attention to my use of those cheap little cans of biscuits. Making them into donuts for my kids on rainy days not only saved my sanity, but brought us closer together as a family and created some of the best memories we share to date. I pray these recipes and ideas help you create some lasting memories with your family while saving time and money in your kitchen. Refer to the Kitchen Tips section, especially the Food Storage section, to learn how to further extend the use and shelf life of many of these staple items.

STAPLES

All-purpose flour

White sugar

Brown sugar

Powdered sugar

Cornmeal (optional)

Baking powder

Baking soda

Shortening

Cooking oil (olive or vegetable)

Powdered milk (optional)

Cider vinegar

White vinegar

Dried beans (legumes) (See **Kitchen Tip #65, #71**)

Cocoa powder

Cereals (oatmeal, cream of wheat, boxed, etc.) (See **Kitchen Tip #126**)

Pasta (elbow, spaghetti, angel hair, etc.)

Real maple syrup

Baker's yeast

SPICES

Salt

Pepper

Vanilla extract

Cinnamon

Nutmeg

Garlic powder (or fresh garlic cloves), garlic salt

Onion powder, onion salt

Tarragon (enhances the flavor of chicken soup & pasta sauces)

(Refer to spice section info)

DAIRY

Milk

Eggs

Butter (margarine)

American cheese (or your favorite brand on sale. To save more money, buy cheese in blocks and freeze what you don't use—see **Kitchen Tip #140**)

Canned biscuits

CONDIMENTS

Ketchup

Mustard

Italian Dressing (I consider this a staple item because it has an extended shelf life in the fridge, and it's great on a salad or a sandwich!)

BACK TO THE BASICS

As the sole supporter of a family of four, I soon discovered that my grocery bill each month was nearly the same amount as my rent. In order to control that bill and keep it consistent each week, I created a weekly meal schedule. On Monday we had macaroni and cheese with hotdogs. Tuesdays was pork chop day, Wednesdays was spaghetti day, Thursday was the one–pan hamburger and tomato soup, mashed potato casserole day, and Friday was fish day or leftover day. My kids didn't like leftovers much, so it was easy to introduce them to fish and seafood this way. And Saturday was pizza day.

I'd buy a square unbaked pizza for four dollars and that was lunch and dinner for the day with maybe a salad and Kool–Aid. Soda pop was too expensive and not part of my budget. On Sundays, I'd make a one–pan pot roast with fresh vegetables or a pot of soup and homemade biscuits or tortillas. The rest of the food bill went to cover their school lunches, laundry supplies, toothpaste, shampoo, school supplies, clothes, etc., and toilet paper. Lots of toilet paper.

I also discovered that buying fresh fruits and vegetables when they were in season was not only a healthier choice, but also a lot cheaper. Chopping and freezing them to use in a meal a few weeks or months later saved time and money as well. Having the food all ready chopped cuts back on meal preparation time, allowing more time to help with homework or to complete other chores when you're on a time crunch. Preserving fresh fruits and vegetables when they are in season saves you not only money, but it also allows you to enjoy many of these foods when they are not available in the grocery stores due to climate changes.

This is one of the ways I survived those hard, hectic times raising my family in the north. I've included a few tips on how to store and freeze many of these foods in the Kitchen Tips and Food Storage sections of this book. Remember, fresh is always best, even if it's fresh frozen.

Making a pot of soup as a main course is another way to save money in the kitchen. I still save steak, pork chop, and chicken bones and freeze them to make a soup broth or stock for later. Boil the bones for about an hour or two in a large kettle of water. I will sometimes let the bones simmer all day while I'm running errands or doing yard work. Use a colander to strain broth or stock to remove bones and toss them in your garden. Your plants love bone meal. Next, add spices, carrots, onion, celery, garlic, and any other vegetable you have handy to your broth or stock, cook for about 20 to 30 minutes more, and you have a hearty meal for your family. All ready frozen, chopped, or canned vegetables will reduce this cooking time. Cook pasta, rice or egg noodles right in the broth for added flavor and to save time as well.

While that's cooking, prepare the pizza dough recipe, and cut into strips to serve as bread sticks with your soup. If you have any leftover pizza dough, cut in strips again, roll in melted butter, then sprinkle with a cinnamon sugar mixture and bake at 400 degrees on a cookie sheet for 10 minutes or until golden. Bake the plain bread sticks for the same time and temperature. Now you have a complete meal with dessert that's hearty, healthy, and easy on the wallet.

Getting back to the basic techniques of cooking and preparing meals with fresh ingredients is now, and will always be, the best bang for your buck and a healthier choice for your family. Making one–pan meals save time in the kitchen with cleanup, and I am still the queen of them today. I've only touched on a few ways that I navigated around my kitchen during our lean times, but I hope it opens your imagination to other possibilities in your own kitchen.

RECIPES OR NOTES

MAKE YOUR OWN

Note: Serving size and calories are based on how I make the recipe and may vary when you prepare them. Also, the cost I've included per recipe is based on prices I pay for these foods in my area, and may be different from what you might pay for them in yours. Regardless, this information should still convince you; it's cheaper to make it from scratch. I also buy food in bulk from places like Sam's Club and Costco's. These stores give you the best bang for your buck when you're raising a growing family or just trying to save money on food costs. Maybe ask for a membership as a Christmas present—it's the gift that keeps on giving for a year!

BREAKFAST
OR LUNCH:

BAKED GRAPEFRUIT

Servings: 2//
calories per
serving: 30//cost
per serving: $0.26

1 grapefruit, halved

Sprinkle each half with brown sugar or

Drizzle with maple syrup

Dot with butter (optional)

Bake @ 400 degrees for 20 minutes. Yum!

CREPES

1 cup flour
2 tablespoons sugar
3 eggs
1 cup milk

Beat eggs until completely blended, add milk, then sugar, and gradually add flour with a whisk (easier and faster), or with a fork until no lumps are visible. Batter should be a thin, runny consistency. Use a small egg pan sprayed with a cooking spray, or wipe a small amount of oil on the cooking surface of your pan to season it. This will keep the first few crepes from sticking to the pan and may need to be repeated throughout the cooking process.

(Crepes should NOT be greasy)

Warm pan on medium heat. Pour a small amount of batter into center of warmed pan and rotate the pan to disperse the egg mixture completely over bottom of pan and up the sides. When batter is no longer clear, gently flip crepe in pan and cook on that side for 30 seconds or so, or until no liquid is visible. Crepes should not be browned. Reduce heat if this occurs. Making crepes takes practice.

I serve them warm, smothered in butter, and sprinkled with powdered sugar, or I wrap them around fresh fruit, or fruit preserve, or cream cheese recipe (or both), and then sprinkle with powdered sugar. I've also reduced the sugar in the recipe by half or more and made them to wrap them around a seafood mixture, and then smother them in a nice white sauce. They can even be folded around lunch meats, cheeses, and breakfast foods like a pita–style sandwich.

The uses and meals you can create with these yummy little crepes are unlimited! Enjoy!

Yields approx. 20 crepes//calories per crepe: 43//cost per crepe: $0.05

It's all about mastering the right pan temperature, along with the right amount of mixture. Some may be thicker than others, but they all taste great and can help create a great breakfast, lunch, or dinner meal on a budget.

CREAM CHEESE FILLING

2 3–ounce packages of cream cheese, softened to room temperature (See **Kitchen Tip #31**)

2 tablespoons powdered sugar (granulated sugars are grainy in texture but can be substituted)

1 egg (optional)

Fruit preserves (fresh or from the jar)

Yields 1 cup// servings per 1 Tablespoon: 16 //calories per serving: 36//cost per serving: $0.13

Beat all ingredients until smooth. With the addition of the egg, this mixture can be baked in pastry puff, cookies, breads, or baked in pre–made crepes, etc. The egg helps bind the mixture together. Cover and bake pre–made crepes with cream cheese and egg mixture at 300 degrees for about 20 minutes or less. Exclude the egg and add fruit preserves to the mixture if not baking.

HOMEMADE GRIDDLE CAKES

PLAIN:

Yields 14 dollar sized cakes// calories per cake: 48//cost per cake: $0.06

1 cup all purpose flour

1 teaspoon baking powder (optional)

½ cup milk ((use buttermilk (See **Kitchen Tip #27**) for traditional buttermilk pancakes or warm water if no milk is available)

1 egg

1 teaspoon vanilla

1 tablespoon melted shortening, lard, or oil

2 teaspoons sugar

Use 2–4 tablespoons melted butter (not margarine) in place of oil and warm the milk or water before adding to flour mixture. Also, add–ins should be at room temperature (See **Kitchen Tip #31**).

NOT PLAIN PANCAKES:

Add to batter:

1 cup shredded apples with ½ teaspoon of cinnamon or;

1 cup fresh blueberries or;

½ cup (or more) mashed bananas or;

½ cup chocolate chips or;

1 cup fresh chopped peaches, plus 2 tablespoons sugar and 1 teaspoon cinnamon (refer to spice section if pregnant) (also may need to reduce milk with this addition, or add more flour to thicken batter.)

Note: If using sugar to sweeten fruits, omit the sugar in the main recipe.

Be aware of the expiration date on the premade pancake mixes. The mold that grows in these outdated mixtures is not visible, but can cause upper respiratory conditions, stomach problems, and/or death if not properly identified and treated. The safest measure is to always make the pancake mix as needed. It's also a lot cheaper.

Mix flour, sugar, and baking powder. Using baking powder makes the cakes raise more than they will without it. Beat eggs and vanilla together, add to dry mixture, and blend thoroughly with wire whisk. Blend in melted shortening last. Add additional liquid if batter is too thick. Cook cakes on a warmed, oiled griddle or fry pan. More oil may need to be added as you work through the batter. Reduce the heat after pan has warmed if griddle cakes brown too fast. They are ready to turn or flip when air bubbles begin to break on the uncooked side. This recipe makes about fourteen, fresh, dollar–size griddle cakes that taste just like the ones Grandma used to make, complete with warm maple syrup on top and using buttermilk gives them the best flavor. Yum! If adding fruit, the measurements do not need to be exact. When you're on a budget, use what you have available to add a little variety to your dishes. Fresh is always best!

FLOUR OR CORN TORTILLAS

1 cup flour or cornmeal (or ½ cup of each for variety)
¼ teaspoon salt (optional)
Warm water to create dough

In medium bowl, add flour (or mixture) and make a well in the center. Add a small amount of warm water to the well and stir with your fingers in a circular motion until flour mixture forms a dough ball. Break dough apart into meatball–size balls. Generously flour work surface, rolling pin, jar, and hands. Press dough balls outward and roll out thin. Cook tortillas in dry (ungreased) iron skillet or pan on both sides until very lightly browned. They cook fast in a hot pan, usually under 2 minutes for both sides. Tortillas can be made larger and baked in ovenproof, slightly greased bowls for use as a salad bowl. Bake these at 400 degrees for about 5–15 minutes, or until tortilla shell is crisp and lightly browned.

These are great for making a quick breakfast, lunch, or dinner sandwich when the bread is all gone! Use a flavored broth instead of water for additional variety.

Yields approx. 12 tortillas//calories per each: flour–33, cornmeal–39//cost per each: $0.02

LUNCH
OR DINNER:

BUTTERNUT GNOCCHI

Note: Substitute same quantity of butternut squash with fresh or canned pumpkin, or acorn squash for variety. To save time and money preparing this dish, buy any or all of these foods from local farms markets when they're plentiful and cheap, bake as directed above, scoop off the peels, store in freezer bags, label, and freeze them. I flatten the squash in the bags and stack them to save room in my freezer. When you're ready to make your gnocchi recipe, completely thaw squash, puree it and prepare as directed above.

3 cups all purpose flour
1 medium butternut squash (yields about 2 ½ cups pureed squash)
¼ – ½ teaspoon nutmeg
½ teaspoon salt
Dash of pepper

Slice butternut squash in half, scoop out seeds and pulp, and place both halves in a baking pan, skin side down in about an inch of water. Cover the pan with aluminum foil and bake squash for about 60 minutes at 400 degrees. Test squash with fork to make sure it's done. Remove from oven, drain most of water from pan and replace foil to allow pan and squash to cool. This makes it easier to remove the skin from the squash. Use a large metal spoon to scoop away rind from squash. Place squash and spices in food processor, blender, or use hand mixer to puree squash. The final product should have the consistency of baby food. Gradually add flour to the squash, one cup at a time, using your hand to fold the flour into the squash to make soft dough that is not sticky. Do not over work the dough. You may not need all three cups of flour to make your gnocchi, so add the last cup sparingly until you achieve a soft dough. The extra flour can be used to keep your counter and knife dusted as you prepare and cut the dough. Gently shape soft dough in large log and slice off a 2 inch piece and roll that piece into a long string about ½ in diameter. Cut the long string into bite–size gnocchi pieces and carefully drop in boiling, salted water in large pot. (See **Kitchen Tip #104**)

Do not over crowd the pot. Gnocchi is done when pieces float to the top. Continue until dough is gone. These gnocchi have almost a sweet, melt–in–your–mouth taste, and is a healthy, quick and easy meal to make. Serve with butter or flavored oil and sprinkled cheese, or with any sauce of your choice.

Yields approx. 90 gnocchi pieces// 6 servings @15 pieces per serving//calories per serving: 350// cost per serving: $0.55

EASY ONE-PAN POT ROAST

Note: The calories and cost of this dish can vary greatly depending on your portion size, the amount of meat consumed and how much you pay for a particular size & cut of meat. This dish always provided another day's meal for my family.

Servings: 4//
calories per serving: beef (4oz serving) 702, pork (4oz serving) 672// approx. cost per serving: $3.45

1 beef or pork roast (size dependent on family needs)

6 potatoes, peeled or not, sliced in half

1 small bag of baby carrots, or 6 large carrots, peeled or not, cut in 2 inch pieces

3 whole onions, peeled and sliced in half

6 parsnips, peeled or not, sliced in half (optional)

4 turnips, peeled and quartered

½ cup prepared mustard

Salt and pepper to taste

In a large roasting pan, add about an inch of water. Rub roast with prepared mustard and place in roasting pan. Place vegetables around the roast and season the roast and vegetables with salt, pepper, and favorite spices to taste. Bake at 350 degrees for about an hour for pork and two hours for beef (or less if you like it rarer). The mustard helps tenderize the meat, hold the spices in place, and gives the overall dish a wonderful flavor.

I love these kinds of meals and love this recipe because there is only one pan to clean! Also see the Easy Breads section for a Yorkshire Bread pudding recipe that can be made from the roast drippings to go along with this meal. It's easy and yummy!

GRANDMA O'S HOMEMADE PIEROGIES

3 cups flour

3 eggs

2–3 tablespoons sour cream (use buttermilk or plain
yogurt as a substitute)

1 cup water (add more if dough is too dry)

Mix flour, eggs, sour cream, and half the water until dough forms. Add remaining water and knead dough gently. Add more water if dough is too dry. Lift and stretch the dough for a few minutes, but do not overwork it. Dough should be smooth on the outside, but a little sticky on the inside. Let dough rest for 20 minutes in closed container in refrigerator or on counter in covered bowl for 30 minutes. Prepare filling while dough rests.

SAUERKRAUT ONION FILLING

1 can (12–14oz) sauerkraut, drained and rinsed well
1 medium onion
½ stick butter
1 tablespoon flour
½ cup chopped sautéed onion (optional)

Chop onions and sauté in butter until translucent. Add flour and drained kraut and cook on low heat for about 15–20 minutes. The kraut should be a little brown and will be more flavorful.

POTATO CHEESE FILLING

Note: Pierogies may float to the surface immediately. Don't panic if they do; simply follow the cooking instructions above.

Yields approx.18 pierogies//
calories per kraut pierogi: 100//
calorie per potato pierogi:126//cost per each kraut pierogi: $0.17//
cost per potato pierogi: $0.28

2 cups leftover mashed potatoes

½ cup cheddar cheese (or favorite flavor)

2 tablespoons flour

2–4 tablespoons butter

½ cup chopped onion

Chop onion and sauté in butter until translucent. Add flour, then mashed potatoes until blended. Fold in cheese.

PREPARING THE PIEROGIES

Form pierogi dough into about 2–inch balls and flatten out in a circular form. Dough should be about a ¼ inch or less thick. Place a teaspoon of kraut or mashed potato mixture on one half and fold over and crimp edges. Using a little milk on these edges before folding them over and crimping will help seal the dough and prevent mixture from seeping out. Gently add prepared pierogies to boiling water. Cook for about 1 ½ minutes each side and do not over crowd the pot. Use wooden spoon to turn pierogies to avoid breakage and use a slotted spoon to gently remove them from pan when they are done. They will float to the surface when they are done.

My grandma took them out of the water and lightly browned them in a skillet with more butter and more onions before serving them. Polacks love butter, and I'm no exception! If she had any dough left, she would fill them with a fruit preserve, or fresh fruit, sauté and lightly brown them in a pan of butter for about 2 minutes on each side, dust them with powdered or granulated sugar, and served them as dessert. Nothing went to waste in her kitchen and this was the best part of our pierogi meal!

HOMEMADE MACARONI & CHEESE

This is a yummy, easy, hearty, and cheap meal to make for a large family. Even if your family is small, this dish freezes well for a future meal. I sometimes add more cheese and buttered breadcrumbs to the top of this dish during the last 5 minutes of baking time for variety. I'll also add cubed ham to the leftover Mac and cheese to create another hearty meal.

Yields 12 cups// calories per cup: 268//cost per cup: $0.49

3 cups uncooked elbow macaroni
2 cups grated or chunks of cheddar cheese
½ –1 cup milk
Salt and pepper to taste

Cook macaroni according to package and your taste. Save some of the boiling liquid and mix with milk. If you don't have milk, just use the water you boiled the macaroni in. Pour enough liquid on the bottom of your casserole dish to cover the bottom. If using shredded cheese, next, place a layer on bottom of oven casserole dish, followed by noodles and seasonings. Continue making layers until cheese and noodles fill your dish. Make sure the top layer is cheese. Pour milk (or boiling liquid) over noodles and cheese to cover half the dish. If using chunks of cheese, add between layers and stir casserole as it bakes to blend mixture. If you don't have enough cheese to cover the top layer, cover dish with aluminum foil to avoid burning noodles and bake as directed. Melted or pads of butter can be added between layers to make the dish even richer tasting. Bake at 350 degrees for about 30 minutes, or until mixture bubbles (See **Kitchen Tip #140**).

ONE PAN CASSEROLE

1 pound hamburger or ground turkey, browned

2 cans green beans, drained

1 can tomato soup

4 medium potatoes, boiled and mashed.

My kids love this dish and made me include this recipe.

Servings: 4// calories per serving: 520//cost per serving: $1.00

In casserole baking dish, mix browned meat with drained green beans and undiluted soup. Bake covered at 350 degrees for 20 minutes or until mixture bubbles. Remove from oven and add mashed potatoes on top of mixture. Return to oven to lightly brown the top of the mashed potatoes. Then add 4 slices of American cheese on top of potatoes. Continue to bake for about 5 minutes or less to melt cheese. If using ground turkey, see **Kitchen Tip #77 and #85** for additional flavor ideas.

EASY BREADS FOR
ANY MEAL:

BANANA BREAD

When I need a chocolate fix, I make this bread and add the semi–sweet chocolate pieces. Yum!

Yields 1 loaf// servings per ½ inch slice: 13 per loaf //calories per serving: 163//cost per serving: $0.15

Calories per serving w/nuts: 193//Calories per serving w/ chocolate pieces: 236//cost per servings: $0.19

1/3 cup shortening

½ cup sugar

2 eggs

1 ¾ cup flour

½ teaspoon soda

1 teaspoon baking powder

½ teaspoon salt

1 cup of mashed bananas, about 3 or 4 bananas (See **Kitchen Tip #49**)

½ cup chopped walnuts (optional) or,

¾ cup mini chocolate chips or ½ cup regular (optional)

1 cup blueberries (optional)

Mix all dry ingredients and set aside. Combine shortening, eggs, and mashed bananas together. Add dry ingredients and mix thoroughly. Fold in walnuts, blueberries, or chocolate chips as desired. Pour into greased loaf or muffin pan (See **Kitchen Tip #19, #32 and #42**) and bake at 350 degrees about 40–50 minutes, or until knife or cake tester inserted in the center comes out clean.

BLUEBERRY BREAD

1/3 cup shortening

½ cup sugar

2 eggs

1 ¾ cup flour

½ teaspoon soda

1 teaspoon baking powder

½ teaspoon salt

1 cup sour cream

1 cup frozen blueberries

Mix all dry ingredients and cut in shortening with pastry blender or use two knives in a scissor fashion to blend these ingredients before adding eggs and sour cream. Mix thoroughly and gently fold in frozen (or fresh) blueberries. Pour into greased loaf or muffin pan and bake at 350 degrees about 40–50 minutes, or until knife or cake tester inserted in the center comes out clean.

Buy fresh blueberries when they are in season and freeze them for use during our long winters in Michigan (See **Kitchen Tips #141, #142, and #19**). To reduce calories, replace 1 cup of sour cream with applesauce.

Yields 1 loaf// servings per ½ inch slice: 13 per loaf//calories per slice: 179// cost per serving: $0.25

CARROT BREAD

I love this recipe and serve this bread with beef or pork roast dinners. Yum!

Yields 1 loaf// servings per ½ inch slice: 13 per loaf//calories per serving: 228 without nuts, 243 with nuts//cost per serving: $0.20 without nuts, $0.23 with nuts

1 cup sugar

¾ cup cooking oil

2 eggs

1 ½ cup flour

1 teaspoon baking soda

1 teaspoon baking powder

1 teaspoon cinnamon

¼ teaspoon salt

1 cup grated carrots

1/4 cup chopped nuts (optional)

Mix eggs well, next add sugar, cooking oil, and finally the combined dry ingredients. When mixture is blended, fold in grated carrots and nuts, and mix thoroughly. Pour into greased loaf or muffin pan and bake at 350 degrees for approximately 55–60 minutes, or until an inserted toothpick or cake tester comes out clean. (See **Kitchen Tip #32**)

LEMON BREAD

½ cup shortening

1 cup sugar

2 eggs

1¼ cup flour

1 teaspoon baking powder

½ teaspoon baking soda

½ teaspoon salt

½ cup milk

2 tablespoons grated lemon peel (also known as lemon zest (See **Kitchen Tip #74**)

½ cup chopped nuts (optional)

I love the taste of lemons in pies, cakes and breads and always have them fresh on hand.

Combine shortening and sugar, then beat in eggs. Add combined dry ingredients alternately with milk until well blended, then fold in the fresh grated lemon peel. Pour into greased loaf, Bundt, muffin, or cake pan and bake at 350 degrees for approximately 45–60 minutes, or until an inserted toothpick or cake tester comes out clean. This recipe can also be made into a lemon cake.

LEMON ICING DRIZZLE

Yields 1 loaf: //
servings per ½
inch slice: 13 per
loaf//calories per
serving: 219//cost
per serving: $0.20

½ cup powdered sugar

3 tablespoons fresh lemon juice (See
Kitchen Tip #61)

Combine the above ingredients and drizzle
over bread, muffins or Bundt cake. Enjoy!

(See **Kitchen Tips #11 and #12**)

YORKSHIRE BREAD PUDDING

2 eggs

1 cup milk

½ teaspoon salt

1 cup all purpose flour

24 Tablespoons of Roast drippings

Reduce recipe by ½ if using a 6 count muffin pan.

Servings: 12//calories per serving: 80//cost per serving: $0.06

In medium bowl with wire whisk, beat eggs until foamy, next beat in milk and ½ teaspoon salt. Gradually add flour until batter is smooth. Spoon roast drippings in 12 count muffin tins, about 2 tablespoons of drippings in each muffin cup, and use pastry brush or fingers to completely coat the inside of each cup. Pre–heat oven to 400 degrees F. and place muffin pan in heated oven for 5 minutes to re–heat drippings. After designated time, remove pan, use pastry brush again to remoisten inside of cups and fill each with about 2 ½ tablespoons of batter. Return to 400 degree oven and bake for 30 minutes.

Loosen pudding from pan and serve warm immediately with roast.

ZUCCHINI BREAD

This bread freezes well and is great for breakfast with a latte or cappuccino.

Recipe ingredients may also be reduced by 1/3 to make a single loaf.

Yields 3 loaves// Servings per ½ inch slice: 13 per loaf//calories per serving: 139// cost per serving: $0.11//

3 cups flour

½ teaspoon salt

3 teaspoons cinnamon

1 teaspoon baking soda

½ teaspoon baking powder

¾ chopped nuts (optional)

1 teaspoon vanilla

3 eggs

1 cup oil

2 cups brown sugar

2 cups grated zucchini, seeds removed

Mix vanilla, oil, eggs, brown sugar, and chopped zucchini together. Add flour, salt, cinnamon, baking powder, baking soda, and nuts. Mix well and pour into three greased loaf pans or muffin tins. Bake at 350 degrees for 60–75 minutes, or until cake tester or toothpick inserted in center of bread comes out clean.

RECIPES OR NOTES

EASY SAUCES FOR PASTA, MEAT, FISH, SEAFOOD, OR VEGETABLES:

BASIC MARINARA (RED) SAUCE

Yields: approx.
3 cups sauce//
calories per cup:
250//cost per cup:
$1.30

1/3 cup olive oil or vegetable oil

2–4 cloves of fresh garlic (crushed and chopped) or 2 tablespoons all ready chopped and diced garlic

2 tablespoons chopped parsley (optional)

1 ½ cup–2 cups chopped, diced tomatoes (or 1 12–ounce can Italian tomatoes with juices)

1 tablespoon fresh oregano, or 1 teaspoon dried, chopped oregano leaves, or 1 tablespoon fresh sage, or 1 teaspoon dried chopped sage

½ teaspoon salt

Dash of pepper

Sauté garlic in oil in large skillet on medium heat for 2–3 minutes. Do not burn garlic, as it becomes bitter tasting. Add parsley, tomatoes, and spices, and bring mixture to a slight boil. You may choose to mash the tomatoes a little with a fork or potato masher to achieve a smoother or pureed sauce consistency, if desired. Reduce heat and simmer sauce for about 30 minutes uncovered, stirring sauce occasionally until it thickens to your desired consistency.

ENHANCING THE MARINARA SAUCE

This is a great, versatile sauce recipe that I use a lot. I change it up a bit by adding fresh, diced vegetables such as squash, peas, mushrooms, corn, olives, steamed or marinated artichokes, etc., to the sauce during its cooking time, and then pour it over the cooked pasta. I add about ¼ cup of water per ½ cup of vegetable added to the sauce to properly cook the vegetables. I may even add more tomatoes. If I'm serving adult guests, I may even substitute a portion of the liquid with red or white wine. Another variation I serve to my family is the creamy red sauce. I'll stir in a cup of cream or milk and 2–4 tablespoons of butter after the cooking time to avoid curdling the cream (or milk) and pour this mixture over pasta. If I have any on hand, I've even added a couple of tablespoons of Gale's Pesto Sauce to the basic recipe to change the flavor further. If your sauce is too thin, refer to **Kitchen Tip #113** for the cornstarch roux. If it's too thick, add more broth or water. How my sauce turns out just depends on what's in the freezer, refrigerator, and the cupboards on the day I'm making it. You can't do much to mess up this recipe and any extra sauce can be frozen for future meals. That's why I love this sauce, and I'm sure you will too!

CHEESE SAUCE

Yields 1 ½ cup
sauce//calories
per 1 Tablespoon
serving: 60//cost
per serving: $0.16

2 tablespoons butter

2 tablespoons flour

¼ teaspoon salt

¼ teaspoon dried mustard

1 cup milk or cream

½ cup grated cheese

Combine butter, flour, and dried mustard in pot on stove. Add milk and salt. Simmer 2–3 minutes, or until mixture is creamy. Remove from heat and stir in grated cheese until melted. Add additional butter by tablespoon if mixture is too thick. Serve immediately with fish, seafood, pasta, or vegetables.

CUCUMBER SAUCE

2 tablespoons butter

2 tablespoons flour

½ teaspoon tarragon

1 dash cayenne pepper

1 cup milk, or ½ cup vegetable broth and ½ cup milk

½ cup chopped, seeded cucumber

Yields 1 cup sauce//calories per 1 Tablespoon serving: 26//cost per serving: $.0.05

Combine butter and flour and cayenne pepper in pot on stove. Add milk, salt, tarragon (if available), and cucumbers. Simmer for about 10 minutes, or until the cucumbers are tender and the flavors have blended. Serve with fish, lamb, or vegetables.

DILL SAUCE

Yields 1 cup
sauce//calories
per 1 Tablespoon
serving: 17//cost
per serving: $0.06

1 tablespoon butter
1 tablespoon flour
¼ teaspoon salt
1 teaspoon minced fresh dill or ½ teaspoon
dried
1 dash of nutmeg
1 cup milk (or fish broth and milk to make
1 cup)

Combine butter and flour in pot on stove,
add milk and remaining ingredients and
whisk or stir over simmering heat for 2–3
minutes. Serve with meat, fish or seafood.

GALE'S HOMEMADE PESTO SAUCE

Puree in blender in this order:

2 cups fresh basil leaves (1 cup of fresh parsley can be substituted for 1 cup of basil)

2–4 tablespoons pine nuts

2 tablespoons fresh grated Parmesan cheese

3–5 cloves of fresh garlic

½ teaspoon fresh lemon juice (bottled is okay, too)

½ teaspoon salt

After mixture is pureed, slowly add:

¼ to ½ cup olive oil (your favorite brand) until completely blended

Note: See spice section for additional information on this herb.

Makes approx. 3/4 cups//cost per batch: $3.25 (store bought), homegrown basil: $1.25

Serve with any pasta variety or freeze mixture for future use. It will keep for months in the freezer if properly stored in airtight containers (See **Kitchen Tip #144**).

Pesto can also be frozen in ice trays covered with plastic wrap. Single cubes can then be used for an individual meal, or added to any sauce for additional flavor.

PIZZA SAUCE

Sauce can also be prepared ahead of time and frozen for future use.

Yields approx. 2 cups sauce (16oz)// calories per cup: 160//cost per cup: $0.99

1 (15 ounce) can tomato sauce

2 cloves of fresh garlic, or 1 tablespoon, minced

1 teaspoon dried basil, or 1 tablespoon fresh basil, minced

1 small onion, minced

1 tablespoon olive oil

Cook onion in oil until translucent, next add garlic, tomato sauce, and basil. Simmer 5–10 minutes to combine flavors. Let sauce cool a bit before spreading over pizza dough.

TARTAR SAUCE

¼ cup mayonnaise or salad dressing (see mayonnaise recipe in "Condiments & Liqueur" section)
1–2 tablespoons sweet pickle relish
1 teaspoon finely chopped onion (optional)

Yields approx. ¼ cup sauce// calories per Tablespoon: 127// cost per ¼ cup: $0.20

Combine all ingredients and let it rest for approx. 30 minutes to blend flavors. Serve with prepared fish dish.

WHITE WINE SAUCE

Yields 1 cup sauce
(8oz)//calories
per 1 Tablespoon
serving: 35//cost
per serving: $.0.06

2 tablespoons butter

2 tablespoons flour

¼ teaspoon salt

1/8 teaspoon pepper

½ cup milk or cream

½ cup white wine

Combine butter and flour in pot on stove. Gradually whisk or stir in milk and seasonings. Stir until well blended and creamy, about 1½–2 minutes, then slowly add wine. Simmer for 2–3 minutes more. Serve with pasta, meat, fish, or seafood. (Substitute ½ cup additional milk or cream in place of ½ cup wine for a plain white sauce.)

RECIPES OR NOTES

DESSERTS:

APPLE FRITTERS

These fritters go great with fresh, hot or cold apple cider. I hope you enjoy them as much as we do!

Yields approx 64 pieces//calories per piece: 19// cost per piece: $0.04

1¼ cup flour

½ teaspoon salt

2 teaspoons baking powder

4 tablespoons sugar

1 egg

½ cup milk

2 tablespoons melted shortening

4 apples (Granny Smith or Macintosh or the like will do) peeled (or not), cored, and sliced in quarters, then quartered again (or quartered smaller if apples are large)

Mix all ingredients, except apples. Batter should be a thick consistency in order to cling to apple piece. Dip each apple piece in batter until coated and gently lower into one or two inches of hot oil in a frying pan or deep fryer. Reduce temperature of oil as needed so browning doesn't occur too fast, allowing the apple to cook. Rotate apple fritters in hot oil to brown on all sides. Remove fritter to paper or clean cloth towel. Sprinkle with powered or granulated sugar immediately and serve warm or cold.

CHOCOLATE FRUIT DIP

¼ cup semi–sweet chocolate bits
1 Tablespoon shortening
Assortment of bit size fruits,
marshmallows, pretzels, etc.

Melt chocolate bits with shortening over double broiler. Serve with bit size morsels immediately. (See **Kitchen Tips #18, #25, and #127**.) Also see **Kitchen Tip #48** for other ideas on using these chocolate bits.

Yields ¼ cup melted chocolate (4 Tablespoons)// calories per 1 tablespoon serving: 180//cost per serving: $0.26

EASY COCONUT FRUIT DIP

Yields approx. 2 cups dip (16oz)// calories per Tablespoon: 49// cost per cup: $1.65

1 package of coconut macaroon cookies

1 8–ounce container of sour cream

1 teaspoon of vanilla

Break up cookies in blender or food processor and set on puree mode, or use cutting blade in the processor to completely crumble. Remove to larger bowl, add sour cream and vanilla, and combine all ingredients. The mixture should be a thick creamy texture that clings perfectly to the fruit when dipped. Serve this dip with any fresh cut fruit of your choice and watch how quickly both disappear! Great for parties!

This is the easiest and best fruit dip I've ever tasted and a hit at all my parties. I sometimes find these cookies in the dollar store for a buck! They also freeze well. If you love coconut, you'll love this recipe! Enjoy!

SNOW VANILLA ICE CREAM

1 large bowl of freshly fallen snow
1 teaspoon vanilla extract
½ cup sugar
½ half & half cream (or any milk)

Catch snow in clean bowl. I use a metal bowl or pot to keep the snow from melting too fast once I bring it in the house. Add cream, vanilla, and sugar. Stir to blend thoroughly and serve immediately. Leftover ice cream can also be frozen. To enhance the flavor of this ice cream, add two teaspoons of your favorite Jell–O gelatin to each cup of ice cream.

I've been eating snow ice cream since I was a little girl. I made it for my children when they were little, and now they will have the recipe to pass on to the generations to come. It's a tasty, refreshing treat for kids of all ages, easy to make, and totally easy on the budget! Enjoy!

My bowl yields about 2 cups of finished ice cream//calories: 440 per 2 cups (with cream)//cost per 2 cups: $0.26

SOUTHERN CHESS PIE

Yields one pie//
servings per pie: 8
slices//calories per
serving: 370//cost
per slice: $0.27

3 eggs

1 ½ cup sugar

1 Tablespoon cornmeal

1 teaspoon vinegar

1 teaspoon vanilla

5 Tablespoons milk

1 stick melted butter (or margarine)

1 unbaked pie crust

Beat eggs first with wire whisk, mixer, or vigorously with fork, mix in vanilla, milk, and vinegar well, then blend in cornmeal. Mix well. Thoroughly blend in melted butter last and pour into unbaked pie crust. Bake @350 degrees for 40–45 minutes or until knife inserted in center comes out clean.

This is an amazing, tasty pie that's easy to prepare and one that my kids always ask me to make during the holidays. The consistency of the filling is similar to that of a pecan pie, only lighter. Actually, I have added pecans to the bottom of the crust before pouring in the filling for variety. This recipe has been in our family forever and our favorite. I'm sure it will quickly become the same in yours! Enjoy!

RECIPES OR NOTES

DOUGH RECIPES:

PIE CRUST

Yields 2 crusts// calories per crust: 800//cost per crust: $0.43

Sift together (or use fork) to evenly mix:

2 cups flour

1 teaspoon salt

Blend with a fork or pastry cutter:

2/3 cup, plus 1 tablespoon shortening (a combination of shortening and butter can be used if desired)

Mixture should resemble coarsely ground cornmeal

ADD TO THIS MIXTURE:

7 – 10 tablespoons ice cold water (one tablespoon at a time; dough should stick together but not be sticky)

Use your hand or a fork to blend flour mixture and water until a ball of dough forms in the center of bowl. Do not overwork dough. Roll dough in wax or cellophane paper and chill for at least 30–45 minutes before attempting to roll out dough. Use a little flour or cornmeal on work surface area and rolling pin (or jar) to keep dough from sticking. Again, do not overwork dough. Yields 2 pie crusts. Great for smaller pie tins and the perfect amount for cobblers or homemade chicken or beef pot pies. Use large size cupcake tins to make individual cobblers or meat pies for variation.

If prebaking crusts to use for a cream–filling recipe, see **Kitchen Tips #4, #20, and #24**. Fruit fillings, see **Kitchen Tip #30**. If using fresh fruits as a filling, refer to **Kitchen Tips #52, #56, and #113**. Cornstarch may be mixed with water as a thickener to reduce calories in recipe if desired. This mixture is also recommended to thicken cold soups.

PIZZA DOUGH

Yields dough for 2 pizzas//calories per pizza dough: 720// cost per each plain pizza dough: $0.31

1 cup very warm water (hot enough to activate yeast, but not burn hands or fingers)

2½ to 3 cups flour (start with fewer amounts and add as needed)

½ teaspoon salt

2 tablespoons cooking oil (olive, vegetable, peanut, etc.)

1 package dry yeast (which equals about 2 teaspoons, or additionally, up to 2 tablespoons can be used for more of a yeasty flavor)

FOR SWEETER DOUGH ADD:

2 tablespoons honey or

2 tablespoons sugar

2 tablespoons maple syrup

Other variations:

2 tablespoons minced garlic (2 tablespoons fresh chopped basil)

By hand: Mix yeast with water to begin its activation and let it stand for 5 minutes or so. Next add sweeteners and spices, (if desired), salt, and oil, and combine all ingredients well. Add flour gradually in small amounts until dough forms a ball. More or less water and flour may be needed to accomplish this. Do not overwork dough. Combine and knead dough no more than about 5 minutes. Dough should not be sticky or too dry. If too dry, add one tablespoon of water at a time to adjust. If dough is too sticky, add flour one teaspoon at a time. Once your ball of dough is formed, transfer to lightly oiled bowl and cover with plastic wrap and set in a warm corner to rise to double its original size. This is usually accomplished in about an hour. Then divide dough in half and roll into balls and place in separate, slightly oiled bowls and cover. Let them rest for about 15 to 30 minutes before shaping them for your favorite pizza or calzones.

Spread pizza sauce on top of dough, followed by meats, fresh vegetables, and cheese of choice, and bake at 400 degrees for about 15–20 minutes.

For a crisper bottom crust, generously oil pizza stone or pan before adding the pizza dough.

Dough can also be prepared ahead of time and refrigerated or frozen until needed.

By bread machine: Add wet ingredients to bread machine first, followed by yeast, then flour and mix on "dough" setting for time allowed per unit.

By food processor: Add wet ingredients to processor first, followed by yeast and water mixture, then flour. Use pastry dough paddle or metal blade (less stressful on machine) to thoroughly mix ingredients to ball shape.

CONDIMENTS &
LIQUEUR:

HERB INFUSED (FLAVORED) OIL

Servings: mixer decides//calories per Tablespoon: 120// cost per serving: mixer decides

Oil (vegetable is the cheapest and makes it taste expensive!)
Fresh herbs (basil, garlic, oregano, sage, thyme, cloves, fennel, marjoram, and dill leaves, etc.)
Wide–mouth jar
Cheesecloth

Tear apart fresh herbs with your hands and loosely fill the jar with them. Completely cover the herbs with oil of choice to fill the jar, place cheesecloth over the opening, and secure with string or a rubber band at the neck of the jar to keep insects out. Set in a warm, sunny corner of your counter and allow the mixture to blend for 2 weeks, stirring daily. Taste test oil after two weeks to determine if it is at the desired flavor. If not, add more fresh herbs and let mixture steep for another week or so. When complete, use cheesecloth to strain herbs from oil while transferring to a usable container. Sunflower, safflower, vegetable, canola, or peanut oils are mild in flavor and work well with more pungent, aromatic spices like oregano, tarragon, basil, sage, cloves, garlic, etc., when the predominant flavor you seek is that of the spice. Olive oils have their own predominant flavor, but do blend well with aromatic spices, especially garlic. These oils can be used to brown meats, fish, or vegetables, or used in marinades and salad dressings. Experiment with different herbs and oils and create your own, healthier blends (See **Kitchen Tips #137 and #146**).

HERB INFUSED (FLAVORED) VINEGAR

Servings: mixer decides//calories per 1 Tablespoon serving: 0//cost per serving; mixer decides

Vinegar (distilled white, wine, or cider variety) Choose the cheapest brand because you're going to make it taste expensive!
Herbs (basil, garlic, bay leaf, dill leaves, lemon time, lemon balm, rosemary, sage, thyme, mint, marjoram, etc.)
Large jar with acid–proof lid

Tear apart herbs and fill jar loosely with them. Add sliced cloves of fresh garlic if desired. Cover herbs and garlic with vinegar that has been warmed (not hot). Close jar and place on warm, sunny area of counter and shake the jar daily. Taste test vinegar mixture to determine if it is at the desired flavor. If not, replace herbs with fresh ones and allow mixture to cure for another week or so until desired flavor. When complete, strain and remove herbs while transferring vinegar to a usable container. A piece of cheesecloth or a small strainer will work well for this step. These vinegar blends can be used in marinades, salad dressings, sauces, or gravies or with vegetables. Create your own unique blends and enjoy the flavor, as well as the savings.

MAYONNAISE

1 egg yolk
1 teaspoon honey
½ teaspoon salt
1/8 teaspoon paprika (optional)
½ teaspoon dry mustard
2 tablespoons vinegar (flavored or white)
1 cup oil

Yields 1 cup–8oz// calories per 1 Tablespoon serving: 125//cost per cup: $0.68

Mix all ingredients in a blender or food processor on high speed, except oil. After first six ingredients are blended, gradually add oil while blending on high speed until creamy texture results. Fold in additional ingredients after mayonnaise is creamy to maintain texture. (See **Kitchen Tip #100** for this perishable item)

This basic recipe can be enhanced by your favorite spice, oil, or vinegar. Let your imagination go and experiment.

SEMI-HOMEMADE
SWEET PICKLES

Note: Reduce this recipe by 1/3 to experiment with regular sized jar (32–48oz.) of dill pickles.

Start with 1 large, cheap jar (1 gallon size) of whole dill pickles. Drain pickle liquid from jar and slice each pickle into round chips or spears, depending on your preference and return pickle pieces to jar.

IN PAN ON STOVETOP, ADD:

½ cup white vinegar

3 cups sugar

1 teaspoon celery seed

1 teaspoon dried mustard

18 whole clove pieces

Cook mix on medium heat and slow boil until sugar is dissolved and flavors are blended, about 10 minutes. Pour mixture over pickles in jar, cover and let stand on counter for about 5 days. Pickles will have a great, crunchy texture with a mild sweet flavor that you just can't get in the store bought variety. Pickles can then be transferred to smaller jars and given as gifts or refrigerated. Enjoy!

Smaller portions of sweet pickles can be made using smaller jars of dill pickles and by cutting the sweetening liquid recipe in half.

You will not believe how crisp these sweet pickles are, and their taste is so good and so unique, you'll make them as Christmas presents and share them with your friends! I do!

KAHLUA LIQUEUR

1 ½ cup firmly packed brown sugar

1 cup white sugar

½ cup instant coffee

2 tablespoons vanilla

2 cups water

3 cups cheap vodka

Combine sugars and water and bring mixture to a boil for 5 minutes to dissolve sugars. Gradually stir in coffee with whisk or spoon, remove from heat and let mixture cool for about an hour. Pour into jug or jar. Add vanilla, and vodka, mix well and seal container. Let mixture age for about two weeks and enjoy responsibly!

My friends and I make this recipe and give the bottles away as gifts. Of course, we always keep a bottle for ourselves too!

RECIPES OR NOTES

PLAY TIME
& CRAFTS:

PLAY DOUGH FOR THE KIDS

Note: I wear a pair of latex surgical gloves (dollar store variety) to mix the color into the dough. Otherwise, see **Kitchen Tip #121**. Store the play dough in airtight container.

Makes 7 cups of play dough// Approximate cost for all this fun: $2.25

5 cups flour

2 cups warm water

2 cups salt

1 to 3 drops food coloring (red, green, blue, yellow, etc.) of choice (Note: Add food color to water prior to mixing if using one color only).

Mix flour, water and salt thoroughly. Add more warm water as needed until dough is easy to handle. Knead dough until it is smooth and easy to handle. Dough can then be separated at this point and color can be added if desired.

This play dough is safe and nontoxic for children, so give them the cookie cutters and the kitchen table (covered, of course) and let 'em go! It will last for a few weeks worth of playtime if properly stored.

NEED ORNAMENTS FOR YOUR CHRISTMAS TREE?

Follow the above play dough recipe, minus the food coloring if desired. When dough is easy to handle and has been kneaded to a smooth texture, roll out dough, using a rolling pin or glass jar, to about ½–inch thickness. Use your favorite cookie cutters for the shapes of your choice or freehand your own design, but don't forget to poke a hole in the top so they can hang from the tree. Bake your designs on a cookie sheet lined with parchment paper for best results (or without) at 300 degrees for about an hour in the middle rack of oven. Adjust to a lower temperature of oven or rack position if bottom browns too quickly. They should become a nice, light, even, tan color. Remove gently to cooling racks. After your dough shapes have cooled they can be painted and designed. Apply a coat of clear shellac over the entire dough piece to preserve your creation.

Approximate cost to make at least 3–4 dozen ornaments: $2.25 (the decoration costs not included–but to save money and also create some memorable keepsakes, use things you may already have around your house like glue, old jewelry, fingernail polish, model paints, permanent ink pens, etc. Get creative and have fun!)

Note: These pieces are for decoration only and should not be eaten. However, you won't die if you do. They also make great Christmas gifts to friends and family!

POPCORN GARLAND

Use microwave or air popped popcorn to make garland for your holiday tree. Start by popping one or two brown paper grocery bags full of popcorn (depending on the size of your tree). To add a little color to your popcorn pieces, place fresh popped corn pieces on a cookie sheet and lightly brush over kernels with a diluted mixture of food coloring(your favorite colors) and water, using a pastry or paint brush. Be careful not to over saturate the kernels. Be sure to separate the colored pieces and let them air dry before placing them in the paper bag(s). Close the bags and put them aside for a week or two until the popcorn turns stale and rubbery. This keeps the kernels from breaking when you begin to string them. Use a needle and heavier gauged sewing thread to create your string of garland.

This is a fun family project, costs pennies to make, and looks great on the Christmas tree along with the homemade dough ornaments! Also check out **Kitchen Tip #150**.

NONTOXIC FINGER PAINTS

1 package of unsweetened, powdered Kool-Aid

1 large container plain yogurt

12 or more sheets of glossy construction paper

Aprons

Surface to create

Small bowls for each artist's colors

Mix Kool-Aid colors with yogurt to create the depth of color desired. Divide colors among the artists and let them create a masterpiece.

Great rainy day project when the kids are stuck indoors! Inexpensive and nontoxic too!

NON TOXIC
TIE-DYED CLOTHING

Note: Vinegar can be optional; however, colors will fade faster without it. Have fun!

Multiple packs of unsweetened powdered Kool-Aid (red, purple, orange, etc.)

Water

Vinegar

Tee shirts, tanks, shorts, etc.

1 large box of rubber bands (small to medium size)

Mix powdered drink mixes to create the colors you desire in small bowls with a small amount of water mixed with 1 tablespoon of white vinegar in each bowl. The amount of water used will determine the depth of color on your final design. Rubber band different sections of the piece of clothing and dip those different sections in the small bowls of colors. You might want to wear a pair of latex or rubber gloves on this project to avoid staining your hands as you ring out some of the excess liquid on each dip of color to avoid bleeds in your design project. The key to your design is the placement of the rubber bands and how many are used. When every section of your clothing has the desired colors, remove rubber bands and hang clothing on a clothesline to dry, and then proudly wear your own creation!

This is a fun, inexpensive family project. On your next family reunion gathering or camping trip, bring some plain white tee shirts along with the Kool–Aid and vinegar and create some memories!

COOKING SEAFOOD
AND FISH

Cooking fish and seafood is a very quick and easy meal to prepare, especially on a busy schedule. Most of us all ready know what fish or seafood we like to eat, have no problem ordering it when we dine out, but wouldn't dare try to cook it at home. This section will hopefully remedy this challenge. It includes a guide to cooking various types of fish based on the thickness and type, as well as a few tips to make sure your home–cooked fish or seafood meal is a yummy experience.

Fish should never have a fishy smell. There is a difference between the smell a freshly caught fish gives off as opposed to the smell a fish gives off once it's been out of the water awhile. A freshly caught fish smells like a fish, but is not offensive. A fish that has been out of the water and on ice for a few days generally has a stronger, more pungent odor, but that doesn't necessarily mean that the fish is spoiled. We encounter this type of fish more in the north because the fresh fish and seafood has to travel a few days to get to us from the coastal areas.

If fish gives off this pungent order, this indicates it needs to be prepared immediately, or thrown out. To determine this, first run the fish under cold water. Next, per **Kitchen Tip #81**, completely cover and soak the fish filet (including shell fish) in a milk bath for up to 15 minutes, turning occasionally. This should remove that pungent odor, as well as prepare the filet to receive spices, rubs, crumbs, etc. Then prepare the fish according to your recipe. If the odor is still pungent after the milk bath and the filet feels slimy or starts to fall apart, toss it to the plants, or feed it to your cat.

Parchment paper is truly a kitchen's best friend. Not only does it enhance the cookie baking process like **Kitchen Tip #39** describes, but it is also the best medium to prepare a tender, steamed filet of fish. The fish will steam perfectly wrapped in a bag fashioned out of parchment paper, and you won't lose any of the tender filets. You can also throw in a few vegetables, some leftover cooked rice, and have a meal in a bag within 10 minutes. It's a great low–calorie, easy clean–up dinner for today's busy family.

To do this, use the sheet pan recommended in **Kitchen Tip #142**. Pour olive oil or any other on hand in the pan to cover entire bottom. Determine the length of parchment needed to cover your filet or meal and dredge both sides of the parchment in the oil. Use your hands to make sure the sheet is covered with oil. This will make folding the paper around the fish or meal easier, help keep the steam from escaping, and keep the paper from burning. If creating a meal in a bag, first place your vegetables, next, cooked rice, then filet of fish, fold and close the sides together, seal both ends, flip over on pan used to oil parchment paper, and bake at 350 degrees for about 10–15 minutes.

Sauces will also enhance a fish or seafood dish and is best added after the fish has cooked. The juices produced by the meal in a bag can be substituted for the liquid called for in a sauce recipe or used to help make up the quantity of liquid needed for the recipe. Homemade sauces start out with a roux, which is a blend of flour and fat. You can use butter, oil, bacon drippings, or lard to make a roux. Butter gives a sauce a much richer, yummier flavor, and more can be added to assist a sauce that may have become too thick or lumpy. To avoid the lumps, prepare your mix of flour or cornstarch with the butter or other fat first as described in **Kitchen Tip #113**.

Fish can be cooked in a variety of ways, ranging from steamed, baked, poached, broiled, grilled, pan–fried, sautéed, or microwave. The cooking times for these fish are approximate and should be gauged against your own cooking medium as well as the size of your filet. A true test of doneness in any fish or seafood variety is color. When the color of the fish is no longer a translucent, watery, or clear color, it's done, unless you're eating sushi. To prevent overcooking, I use the "finger" test. I test the center of the fish after it's been cooking on the second side for about a minute. The center should be almost firm, not hard. Remove fish from hot pan to stop the cooking process to prevent overcooking.

Note: The FDA recommends that fish such as shark, swordfish, king mackerel, albacore tuna, and tilefish should not be eaten by expectant mothers as they contain high levels of mercury called methyl mercury that may harm the fetus's developing nervous system. Women of childbearing age and young children should also limit their servings of these fish types to no more than twice a week.

Fresh shrimp need far less time and can become hard and chewy if overcooked. If the shrimp are pink, they are already cooked and only need a minute or less of cooking time to thaw and reheat when using this variety in a recipe. If they have that translucent, clear appearance, they only need a minute or two of cooking time to turn pink, indicating they are done.

The same applies to crab legs. If you purchase king crab or snow crab legs and they are frozen pink, they have already been cooked and only need a small amount of cooking time, usually 2–5 minutes is all, before they're ready to eat.

Scallops, squid (calamari), and conch also cook quickly and will become tough and chewy if over cooked. Again, the best test is a visual one, along with touch, to prevent over or undercooking your fish or seafood choice.

COOKING TIMES FOR
FISH & SEAFOOD

COOKING FRESH AND SALTWATER FISH	COOKING TIME IN MINUTES (PER 1 INCH THICKNESS)
FIN FISH	
Amberjack	10 (5 on each side)
Black Cod	10 (5 on each side)
Bluefish	9 (4.5 on each side)
Butterfish	10 (5 on each side)
Catfish	10 (5 on each side)
Cod	10 (5 on each side)
Flounder	10 (5 on each side)
Grouper	12 (6 on each side)
Haddock	10 (5 on each side)
Halibut	8 (4 on each side)
Lake Perch	8 (4 on each side)
Mackerel	9 (4.5 on each side)
Mahi-Mahi	10 (5 on each side)
Marlin	8 (4 on each side)
Monkfish	12 (6 on each side)
Mullet	9 (4.5 on each side)
Ocean Cat	10 (5 on each side)
Ocean Perch	10 (5 on each side)
Pollock	10 (5 on each side)
Pompano	9 (4.5 on each side)
Rockfish	10 (5 on each side)
Salmon	9 (4.5 on each side)
Sea Bass	12 (6 on each side)

List continues to next page

Shad	10 (5 on each side)
Shark	9 (4.5 on each side)
Smelt	8 (4.5 on each side)
Snapper	12 (6 on each side)
Sturgeon	9 (4.5 on each side)
Swordfish	8 (4 on each side)
Tilefish	12 (6 on each side)
Trout	9 (4.5 on each side)
Tuna	6 (3 on each side)
Walleye Pike	8 (4 on each side)
Whitefish	10 (5 on each side)

*Bake fish at 325 degrees.

*Poach or steam fish in covered pan on stovetop or oven in small amount of liquid until meat flakes apart.

COOKING SEAFOOD	
SHELL FISH	COOKING TIME IN MINUTES
Bay Scallops	1.5
Clams	5–7 until open
Crab (live)	3-4 (or until pink)
Crawfish	2–3 min. (or until pink)
Lobster	12 for first pound, 6 for each additional pound (lobster will be pinkish red in color)
Mussels	3–4 until open
Octopus	1-1.5 hours (whole)
Oysters	2–3 until edges curl
Sea Scallops (large)	4-5, or until no longer translucent
Shrimp (large)	4 (or until pink)
Shrimp (medium)	3 (or until pink)
Squid Rings	1–1.5

*Clams and mussels can be steamed in about half a cup of your favorite white wine and a few cloves of chopped garlic for flavor.

150 KITCHEN TIPS

The following list of tips and food information will introduce you to foods that have multiple uses, how to pick out a fresh loaf of bread from the supermarket, make gravies without lumps, make cheap cuts of meat taste expensive, and so much more. Kitchen techniques, ideas, and information that will help make baking or meal preparation a pleasant and successful experience on a shoestring budget.

BAKING TIPS:

1. Expand frosting tip. Nearly double the size of a store–bought container of icing by whipping it with an electric mixer for a few minutes. This not only allows you to ice more cakes or cupcakes, but also reduces the calories per serving. This icing can also be microwaved and reduced to liquid form to drizzle over a Bundt, coffee cake, or candy bark and hardens perfectly when cooled.

2. Reheat refrigerated bread. To warm refrigerated muffins, biscuits, pancakes, etc., place them in the microwave with a cup of water. The moisture from the cup of water will keep the breads moist and reheat faster.

3. Measuring cups. Easily remove sticky or greasy substances like shortening, lard, peanut butter, etc., from your measuring cup by first filling it with hot water for a minute or so, dump the water, then add your ingredient to the cup.

4. Have you ever baked a pie or a loaf of bread and the piecrust edge or the top of your bread is perfectly browned but the pie or bread is not quite done? Use a piece of aluminum foil to cover the top of the bread or tear off strips and cover the edge of the crust and continue baking until done. The aluminum foil protects the crust or bread top from continuing to brown.

5.   The truth about flour is that it all comes pre–sifted, so you don't really need to do it again at home. Therefore, it's a good idea to use a little less flour in your recipe as a good bit of air is all ready mixed in during the factory sifting process, which puffs up the volume of the product. Sifting is great for blending and removing any lumps from other dry ingredients added to a recipe.

6.   When beating egg whites for meringue, make sure they are fairly stiff before adding the sugar. If you add the sugar too soon, it increases the time you have to beat the egg whites in order to get the consistency needed for your meringue recipe.

7.   Egg whites will also have more volume if you let them come to room temperature before beating them stiff for a meringue recipe (See **Kitchen Tip #31**).

8.   Heavy whipping cream (not half & half or coffee cream) will create more volume if not only the cream is cold, but the bowl and beaters are chilled as well. A chilled metal bowl works best.

9.   Every time you open your oven door to check on your dish, the temperature inside drops by about 25 degrees.

10. If sweet cream is just starting to sour, add a pinch of baking soda to restore the sweetness.

11. Adding a pinch of baking powder to powdered sugar icing will help it stay moist and prevent the icing from cracking.

12. Homemade icings won't be grainy if a pinch of salt is added to the sugar.

13. If eggs are beaten first, then added to your cake recipe; it won't make the batter too thick.

14. Cookies will stay moist in a jar if a fresh slice of bread is added to the jar. Replace the bread with a fresh slice when the previous one hardens until cookies are gone.

15. To limit cholesterol and calorie intake, add two beaten egg whites to your favorite recipes per each whole egg called for.

16. To preserve the creamy texture of frozen cheesecakes, thaw in your refrigerator for at least 12 hours before serving.

17. Dipping a cookie cutter in warm salad oil before cutting into dough will produce a cleaner cut and crispier cookie.

18. Add a pinch of salt to chocolate dishes to enhance the chocolate flavor.

19. When a recipe calls for you to "fold" in specific ingredients, use a spatula or wooden spoon to gently lift the ingredients from the bottom of the bowl and fold them into the ingredients on top of those on the bottom, using no more than 5 or 6 hand strokes to do

so. "Folding" traps air in the mixture. The larger the utensil used to 'fold' ingredients together will minimize the number of hand strokes needed to blend the mixture. Never stir or use a metal spoon to fold ingredients. For the best results when "folding" in specific ingredients, place the heavier or more dense (thicker) ingredients in the bowl first, then add the lighter ingredients on top. Doing it this way adds more air during the folding process, which results in a fluffier end result in your recipe.

20. To keep an unfilled piecrust from shrinking or puffing up in spots, place a sheet of aluminum over the piecrust and fill with rice or beans and bake as directed. The best part is you can reuse the rice and beans.

21. Create fluffier omelets, quiche, or scrambled eggs by adding a pinch of cornstarch and a tablespoon or two of water prior to beating eggs by hand, with a mixer, or in a blender. The more the eggs are whipped, the fluffier the end product will be.

22. To determine if an egg is fresh, place it in a cool pan of salted water. If the egg sinks, it's fresh. If it floats to the surface, it isn't and shouldn't be eaten.

23. You can tell if an egg is hardboiled or raw by either spinning it or by putting it in a bowl of cold water. The egg that's raw will warble, but the egg that's boiled will spin beautifully. In the water, the egg

that's boiled will float, but the raw egg will stay on the bottom of the bowl.

24. To prevent the bottom of a piecrust from getting soggy when using creamy fillings, try buttering the dish prior to placing the piecrust in the pan.

25. Before melting chocolate in a pan or double broiler, rub the pan or double boiler with butter first and the chocolate won't stick.

26. To eliminate "weeping" meringue, turn oven off, and leave pie in oven until it cools. You may need to leave the oven door open for 5 minutes or so to reduce the temperature in the oven, then close door and let pie rest until it cools. A warm dry pantry is also a good place to let the pie rest.

27. To make buttermilk, add one tablespoon of white vinegar to 1 cup of whole milk.

28. One teaspoon of baking powder equals 3/8 teaspoon of cream of tartar. One teaspoon of baking powder also equals ¼ teaspoon baking soda plus one teaspoon of cream of tartar (see "Equivalents" section).

29. One cup of honey equals 1¼ cup of sugar plus 1 cup of water.

30. To keep fruit pies from spilling over during baking, always make sure your filling is cold before pouring it into your crust. Also, lightly moisten the rim of the bottom crust with water or milk before adding the top crust. Press the top and bottom crust together

and bake as the recipe directs. This stops the filling from oozing out between the crusts.

31. Cakes turn out best when all ingredients are used at room temperature, including eggs, and the batter is not over–mixed. Room temperature is usually accomplished in about 45 minutes. Cook in predetermined oven temperature in center of oven on center rack to produce a level cake product, cookies slightly off center and a little higher in oven. It is also a good tip to zigzag a knife through the batter of your cake to break any air pockets that may be present before baking.

32. Tin pans that are bright and shiny work best for baking cakes, breads, etc., as they warm quickly, reflect the heat, and allow the product to brown delicately.

33. Place a slice of apple in a fresh loaf of bread or in a cake storage container to keep both moist.

34. Measuring ingredients accurately is essential to a successful baked product, be it a cake, cookies, or bread. The best way is to overfill the flour, sugar, etc., and use the back of a table knife to level off the extra ingredient. In the case of brown sugar or shortening, always pack the measuring cup using the back of the spoon to make sure there are no gaps and use the back of a knife to level off the extra.

35. Egg yolks separate from their whites easier when they are brought to room temperature first. Egg

whites also can be beaten to higher volumes at room temperature (See **Kitchen Tip #31**)

36. Egg whites will not reach full volume if there is a speck of yolk (or fat) in them. Remove any yolk with a piece of eggshell (be careful not to leave any behind) or paper towel before beating.

37. Fresh yeast should be stored in the refrigerator in an airtight container when not in use, but should be used in a recipe at room temperature for best results. (See **Kitchen Tip #31**)

38. When rolling cutout cookies, dust your board with a mixture of confectioner sugar and flour for crispier cookies.

39. When baking cookies or short cakes, etc., use parchment paper to line the cookie sheets. Spray or oil the cookie sheet first to hold the parchment paper in place. The cookies will cook evenly and won't burn and clean up is easy between batches.

40. Use applesauce in place of oil in your baking recipes, be it cakes, cookies, or breads—a great way to cut cholesterol as well as calories.

41. Using a solid vegetable shortening, be it regular or butter flavored, in place of butter in a cookie recipe will produce a crispier cookie.

42. If a homemade loaf of bread falls during baking, too much liquid was used. If a loaf of bread turns out small, dense, and heavy, too little liquid was used.

To correct this for the next loaf, use 1 tablespoon more of flour to keep bread from falling, or add 1 more tablespoon of liquid to avoid the small, dense loafs. If using a bread machine, this can be corrected within the first 15 minutes of the machine's cycle.

43. The use of peanut oil in homemade bread recipes will keep the breads fresher longer.

44. To prevent egg mixtures from curdling or becoming lumpy when using a double boiler, never let the water in the lower pan touch the upper pan. Also, add cold egg mixtures to hot mixtures gradually to keep the eggs from scrambling or cooking. (See **Kitchen Tip #127**)

45. Substitute 3 tablespoons of carob or cocoa powder, plus 2 tablespoons of water or milk for each unsweetened chocolate square called for in a recipe.

46. Substitute ¾ cup of honey or molasses and reduce the liquid called for in the recipe by ¼ cup instead of using 1 cup of refined sugar.

47. Use shortening in place of oil in a bread recipe for a crispier outer crust.

48. Mix two tablespoons of white corn syrup to 1 cup chocolate pieces to create a perfect icing for brownies, cupcakes, candy bark, or candy pieces. Melt chocolate pieces with corn syrup in double boiler or microwave. Do not scorch or boil chocolate. Stir and use a spoon to drizzle melted chocolate mixture over baked items or candies. Extra tip: add additional candies or decorations to icing before it cools.

RECIPES OR NOTES

FRUIT & VEGETABLE TIPS:

49. For bananas that are too ripe and too brown or mushy to eat, place them, skin and all, in a zip lock freezer bag and freeze them for future use in a bread, cake, or muffin recipe. Remove peels while bananas are still frozen and place in bowl, as they will already be mashed when they thaw.

50. To maintain all the nutrients in potatoes, sweet potatoes, turnips, rutabagas, etc., boil them with the skins on for approximately 25–30 minutes, or until fork inserts easily into the vegetable. Then drain the water, remove the skins and dice the vegetables according to the recipe you're preparing.

51. Mashed potatoes will have a whipped cream look if you add hot milk to them before mashing instead of cold.

52. Do not add sugar to stewed fruits until they have boiled at least 10 minutes. This cooking time allows the fruit to release their own natural sugars, which will reduce the amount of additional sweeteners needed.

53. Potatoes will take on a golden appearance when sprinkled with a little flour before frying.

54. To maintain the rich color of vegetables, add a pinch of baking soda to the water you cook them in instead of salt, as salt tends to make some vegetables tougher as they cook.

55. To prevent onions from burning your eyes while peeling or slicing, hold them under cold running water while peeling or slicing them.

56. Add a ¼ teaspoon of baking soda to cranberries when cooking and they will require less sugar (or maple syrup, see **Kitchen Tip #125**) to sweeten them.

57. Ripen avocados and tomatoes quicker by placing them in a brown paper bag on your counter.

58. If you don't want to wait for your avocado to ripen the long way using the paper bag method (See **Kitchen Tip #57**), ripen them quickly in the microwave on low power for 2–4 minutes.

59. You can peel fruits and tomatoes easily by placing them one at a time in about one cup of hot water and microwave them for 30–45 seconds on high. Peels should remove easily. You can also place them into a pot of boiling water on the stove (enough to cover the food item) for three minutes or so to easily remove the peels. This process is called blanching.

60. Plump raisins or other dried fruit in the microwave by placing fruit in a bowl with a couple of teaspoons of water, cover and cook on high for approximately 30–90 seconds, or until fruit plumps to your liking. This can also be accomplished in a pan on top of the stove with about 1/8 to 1/4 of a cup of water (or liquid of your choice), depending on the amount of fruit, in a covered pot until fruit absorbs the liquid

and plumps. This can also be done in the oven by washing fruit, then spreading them out in a covered pie plate or dish and bake slowly at 350 degrees until they rehydrate and plump.

61. Lemons warmed or at room temperature produce more juice than when they are cold (See **Kitchen Tip #31**).

62. Use the inside of a banana peel to relieve the itching of mosquito bites. The inside of the peel will also take scuff marks off shoes.

63. Leftover mashed potatoes or instant potato flakes can also be used to thicken soups and sauces.

64. To keep artichokes from turning brown while cutting and removing the outer layers to access its "heart," occasionally dip it in a mixture of water and lemon juice during the process.

65. The term "legumes" is used to refer to vegetables that bear their fruit or seeds in pods, such as peas, beans, lentils, etc., and are usually found in dried form.

66. Use a small amount of brown sugar, white sugar, or maple syrup to taste to eliminate the sharp flavor and acidic content of tomato sauce. Add a dash of cinnamon or a cinnamon stick to the sauce while cooking for additional flavor.

67. To keep dried, sticky fruits from sticking to your knife or scissors while chopping or dicing, coat the

blades with flour or powdered sugar first and during the chopping or dicing process.

68. Planning on making stuffed cabbages? Freeze the head of cabbage first. On the day you plan to make the cabbage rolls, remove cabbage from the freezer and let it thaw. Then core as usual, and the leaves separate easily and are pliable to wrap around your filling. No more burned hands or fingers boiling it the old fashioned way!

69. To reduce the salty taste from over–salted soups or stews, beans, etc., drop a few slices of raw potatoes in the pot and remove before they overcook, as they will dissolve and act as a thickener. Continue adding slices until you get the desired flavor.

70. To keep potatoes fresher longer and to stop them from developing sprouts, add an unpeeled apple to their bag or bin. Replace with fresh apple as needed.

71. The trick to cooking a perfect pot of beans is in the boiling process. Soak dried beans according to the package. Fill pot with water to cover beans plus two inches, season, and bring to a boil. Then reduce heat immediately to medium low so that the boil process is barely visible. Stir occasionally with a wooden spoon or heatproof spatula. Using these types of utensils will keep the beans intact and cooking them slowly will keep them from bursting. They should be cooked in about 1–2 hours (See **Kitchen Tip #65**).

72. Buy bags of fresh mini carrots when they are in season and cheap and freeze them. Carrots freeze well, but lose their crunchy texture, but cook quickly and perfectly in soups, stews, or stuffing. Cut or dice them while frozen. This also works well for fresh broccoli.

73. When preparing dried fruits for use in a recipe, adding a tablespoon or two of fresh lemon juice and a pinch of lemon zest to the stewing liquid or water will enhance the flavor of the fruit. Fresh is always best, but dried will do, too.

74. Lemon zest is harvested from the bright yellow outer layer of the lemon. Use a lemon zest knife or a serrated knife to gently scrape off this bright yellow layer just up to the white skin. The white skin is bitter and should not be used. This part of the lemon contains the fruits' essential oils and has lots of flavor. Finely chopped lemon zest can be used to enhance almost any recipe, especially the lemon bread recipe.

75. To pick the freshest coconut, choose one between the months of October to December, make sure the 'eyes' are not weeping and that there is no mold visible on the fruit. To harvest the juice or 'milk', use a clean nail to puncture one of the eyes, and drain into measuring device. To harvest the meat, use hammer and tap on the widest part of the coconut to crack its shell. Pry out coconut meat and eat raw or it can be shredded and toasted @350 degrees Fahrenheit for 20–30 minutes or until lightly toasted.

MEAT, FISH, & SEAFOOD TIPS:

76. The secret to cooking bacon is to start it in a large, cool pan and cook it slowly on medium to low heat. It will cook thoroughly in its own grease without burning and not shrink as much if you cook it this way.

77. Enhance the flavor of steaks, hamburgers, pork, turkey, and chicken with liquid smoke. I use either hickory or mesquite flavor. Look for it in the condiment section of grocery store. It makes cheaper cuts of meat taste expensive!

78. Be careful when you barbecue fatty meats. The fat that drips on the coals or burners is burned as pyrrolated hydrocarbons. This substance flares onto your meats and can equal the cancer causing agents found in about 600 cigarettes. It's best to grill low–fat meat, or trim most of the fat off your meats before grilling. It also helps to put foil on the grill before cooking fatty meats to prevent flames from flaring onto your foods while cooking.

79. Score has a different meaning in the kitchen. You score meat, fish, or vegetables by cutting narrowing gashes part way through the outer surface of the food. This will allow larger cuts of meat, fish, or vegetables to cook faster or evenly, plus you can insert your favorite spices, herbs, or cloves of garlic in these scores to add additional flavor to your dish.

80. The term "sear" in the kitchen usual refers to the preparation of meats. This is accomplished by quickly browning both sides of the product over high heat in a small amount of oil. This seals in the natural juices of the product during the remaining cooking period of your recipe.

81. Soaking fish or seafood that is not fresh caught in a milk bath, or covering the fish with milk for about 15 minutes will reduce the fishy, pungent odor and flavor of the product (see "Cooking Fish" section).

82. Papaya juice can be used as a meat tenderizer. Cover meat with juice and soak for 30 minutes to an hour, turning occasionally.

83. The next time you make meatloaf, try baking it in muffin tins instead of a loaf pan. The individual meat loafs are easy to freeze and ready to go for the busy family or single professional.

84. Make your own coconut encrusted chicken, fish, shrimp, etc., by dusting food in cornstarch (mixed with spices, if desired), then dredge food in beaten egg whites, then roll in coconut and bake or fry as directed. If frying, use at least 2 inches of oil and do not over crowd the pan to avoid over browning your food item.

85. To make ground turkey taste like ground hamburger without the extra calories, add about ¼–½ cup of Worcestershire sauce to the meat and coat

completely. Then brown meat for use in spaghetti or pasta sauce or mold raw meat into meatloaf (See **Kitchen Tips #83 & #87**).

86. When freezing freshly caught fish or market fresh fish, fill freezer bag with fresh tap water, enough to cover the fish, before freezing. It's best to freeze each fish filet separately and lay flat and stack each bag on the other in the freezer. The fish will taste just as fresh and moist as the day you caught it or bought it.

87. Add variety to ordinary meatloaf by adding a couple of hardboiled eggs to it. Prepare meat according to your recipe and place half in loaf pan. Next add two or three hardboiled eggs on top and cover them with the rest of the meat mixture, form your loaf and bake as directed. If using muffin tins, fill cups halfway, and place a slice of hardboiled egg on top, then cover with remaining meatloaf. Optional: Mix one can of tomato soup and one can of whole tomatoes, diced (or just 2 cans of undiluted tomato soup stirred well, or 1 can undiluted tomato soup mixed with ½ cup ketchup) to top of loaf style meatloaf and bake at 350 degrees for about 30–40 minutes. Yum!

88. Game birds are lean and lower in fat and calories than chicken or turkey, with the exception of duck. Most birds like duck, pigeon, squab, and pheasant have dark meat and can be cooked and eaten safely at rare temperatures.

89. Quail and partridge are white meat fowl, and should be cooked well but not dry. The best way to avoid this is to cover these types of birds with a wet, buttered cloth (cheesecloth will do) while baking, and baste occasionally with melted bacon grease, peanut oil, or butter. (Make sure to remoisten the cloth as needed to keep it and your bird from burning.)

90. Pheasant meat tends to be tougher on older birds. The best way to tell the age of the bird is by its last big wing feather. If the feather is pointed, it's a young bird. If the feather is rounded, it's an older bird, and the meat may need to be parboiled prior to roasting or baking to help tenderize it. These older birds make excellent pheasant and dumplings, or pheasant noodle soup. Yum!

91. Meats such as beef, pork, and ribs can be thawed and refrozen safely. Chicken or other fowl thawed in the refrigerator can be refrozen. Thawed fish should be cooked immediately and should never be refrozen.

92. Freeze steak, pork chop, and chicken bones to make homemade beef or chicken broth for soups or stuffing. It's cheaper and healthier than buying the premade broth.

93. Add chopped, heated pistachio nuts to curried rice for added flavor. Makes an excellent side dish for a wild game meal.

RECIPES OR NOTES

_____

_____

_____

_____

_____

_____

_____

_____

_____

_____

_____

_____

_____

_____

_____

_____

_____

Kiss the
Cook!

OTHER HELPFUL TIPS & FOOD INFORMATION:

94. Have you ever wondered which loaf of bread is the freshest loaf at the grocery store? Pay attention to the color of the twist tie. Bread is delivered fresh on Monday, Tuesday, Thursday, Friday, and Saturday.

     a. Monday = Blue
     b. Tuesday = Green
     c. Thursday = Red
     d. Friday = White
     e. Saturday = Yellow

95. Therefore, if you're buying bread on Thursday, you want to buy a loaf of bread with a red twist tie instead of a white twist tie. The bread with a white twist tie has been on the shelf for almost a week.

96. Fruit flies. Get rid of pesky fruit flies by filling a small glass with about a half inch of apple cider vinegar and 2 drops of dishwashing liquid and set it on your counter. The flies will be drawn to the vinegar and won't survive after they take a drink of this mixture. These little flies are also attracted to wine. So if you're a wine lover, pour a small amount of red or white wine into the lid of an unused jar, set it on your counter and they'll also drown taking a drink.

97. Ants in your kitchen? Put small piles of cornmeal in jar lids where you notice ants. Ants can't digest cornmeal, so when they take it back to their nests,

it will eventually kill them. It may take a week or so to get rid of them, but it's effective and won't harm children or pets in the process.

98. An excellent, healthier thickener for soups is oatmeal. It adds richness and flavor. Grind the oatmeal in a food processor or blender and add to soup by tablespoon until desired thickness results. This ground mixture can also be used in a cookie recipe instead of, or along with flour.

99. The grains of rice will remain white and separated if you add one teaspoon of lemon juice to each quart of water used to cook the rice.

100. The coldest part of any refrigerator is the top back shelf.

101. A piece of raw spaghetti works great to light birthday candles.

102. Mayonnaise will kill lice and condition your hair in the process. Saturate dry hair with mayonnaise and rest 10 to 20 minutes. Use a fine comb through hair occasionally during the wait and wash with regular shampoo. (See "Make Your Own" section).

103. Creamy peanut butter will take the scratches out of music CDs. This really works. Apply the creamy peanut butter with a Q–tip in a circular motion over the entire CD. Then wipe off all the peanut butter in the same circular motion using either a Kleenex tissue (this brand is less abrasive) or a coffee filter. If the CD

still skips, repeat process until it doesn't. Make sure to burn a copy if it's a favorite! You'll be amazed.

104. Two or three tablespoons of butter added to the boiling water while cooking potatoes, spaghetti, rice, noodles, or similar starches will keep the water from boiling over. Don't want the extra calories? Adding an ice cube or two to the boiling water continually as it rises will do the same thing.

105. To remove tea and coffee stains from glass and metal pots, wet the pots and pour on a layer of salt and wipe clean with a dishrag or paper towel.

106. Ice cubes made from lemonade will give your ice tea or cocktails an added punch.

107. If you add an instant beverage to heated water immediately, you break the surface tension and cause the water to bubble over the cup. This is especially true of microwave water or milk. To avoid this, wait 5–10 seconds before adding the instant beverage to the liquid.

108. To freshen chips and crackers that have softened or staled, try microwaving them for about 15–30 seconds on high (depending on the power of your microwave) and let them stand for 2–3 minutes afterward. They should taste fresh and crisp again.

109. You can dry fresh herbs in the microwave by placing them on a paper towel and microwave them on high for 2–3 minutes, or until herbs are dry. Again,

the time depends on how powerful your microwave is. If you don't have a microwave, tie your herbs in a bundle at their stems with a piece of string, and hang them upside down on an indoor clothesline away from direct sunlight until they dry.

110. Make your own breadcrumbs in the microwave by placing crumbled bread pieces on a paper towel and cook for 6–7 minutes, occasionally stirring them around to evenly toast them. Again, cook time depends on your microwave power.

111. Soften a hard brick of brown sugar in the microwave by placing it in a dish with a slice of apple or fresh slice of bread and cook on high for about 30–45 seconds, stirring once or so. If you don't have a microwave, place brown sugar in oven friendly dish and bake at 400 degrees for 5 minutes or so until sugar heats up and begins to break apart.

112. To create perfect hardboiled eggs without cracking the shells, start eggs in cold water in pot on high heat. Remove pot from burner when eggs first begin to boil, cover, and let them stand for at least 10 minutes. Then replace hot water with cold and peeling them should be a snap and the yolks shouldn't have that green ring around its outer edge.

113. To thicken sauces and gravies, combine and blend equal parts of butter and flour, also called a roux, into a paste and refrigerate until solid. If using cornstarch, use one tablespoon butter to 1/2 tablespoon corn-

starch. The chilled roux mixture will slowly thicken your product without lumping, and any extra can be frozen or refrigerated for future use. Stir in 3 tablespoons of this mixture per 1 cup of liquid to thicken your product (See **Kitchen Tips #63 and #98**).

114. Herbs and spices do have an expiration date, which is usually in about a year or so from the date of purchase if the bottle doesn't specify one. The best test is to smell them or pour a small amount in the palm of your hand and rub the spice into your hand with your fingers. The friction and warmth of your hand and fingers should stimulate the oils or aroma of the spice, similar to a hot pan or liquid. If they've lost their aroma, toss them.

115. The natural wood spring–clamp style clothespins can be used to close unused bags of chips, crackers, pastas, bags of coffee, etc., instead of the plastic clips. They can also be clipped onto your cookbook to keep it open to the page your recipe is on. And the best part is you can buy a package of about 48 clothespins for a buck at the dollar store. Then you can use the leftover clips for your laundry. Truly a multitasking little device.

116. Use hydrogen peroxide to remove red wine stains from clothing, carpets, and teeth. For clothing and carpets, slightly wet the stained area with water first, then saturate the stain with undiluted peroxide and let it work on the stain for a few minutes. Repeat

the process until stain is gone. Do not wash and dry the garment until stain is gone. When stain is gone, rinse with clear water. To remove red wine stains from your teeth, swish a small amount of peroxide in your mouth and hold for 3–5 minutes, then spit it out. DO NOT SWALLOW the peroxide. Immediately rinse your mouth with fresh water (See **Kitchen Tip #122**).

117. To microwave small amounts of food such as dough-nuts, butter pats, chocolate pieces, biscuits, etc., place a cup of water in with the food to absorb the excess heat energy and avoid overcooking your food item.

118. Honey is the only food that doesn't spoil or have an expiration date. If it crystallizes or hardens in its container, place the container in very warm water for a few minutes to liquefy again. It's good to the last drop.

119. A turkey baster works great to remove excess liquid or grease from large pots and pans. It looks like an eyedropper for a giant.

120. Ever wondered about the term "part" or "parts" in a recipe, as in use 8 parts water, 2 parts vinegar, etc.? This term means that the same measuring instru-ment is used for all the ingredients in the recipe, such as 8 cups of water with 2 cups of vinegar, or 8 tablespoons water with 2 tablespoons vinegar, etc.

121. Use cooking oils to remove food coloring from your hands. Pour a small amount in the palm of your

hands and rub together. Remove oil and coloring with paper towel or dry rag and repeat process until coloring is gone.

122. Use salt to remove red wine or colored beverage spills on carpets. The salt will absorb the excess liquid and can be vacuumed away. If stain remains, see **Kitchen Tip #116**.

123. Use onion flavored chip dip instead of sour cream on your baked or boiled potatoes. The chip dip has more flavor (if you like onions) and has the same amount of calories as plain sour cream.

124. The next time the glass part of a light bulb breaks off in the socket, cut a raw potato in half and press one half over the metal rim and filament of the broken bulb and twist out as usual.

125. Pure maple syrup is an excellent natural sweetener and loaded with vitamins and minerals. The grade B (darker) variety is packed with sodium, potassium, calcium, magnesium, iron, copper, phosphorus, sulfur, silicon, vitamins A, B1, B2, B6, B5 (pantothenic acid), as well as vitamin C. The grade A variety has a lesser quantity of these nutrients, is less expensive, but is still a much healthier choice over refined sugars. So the next time you make hot cereal, or need to sweeten tart fruit, reach for the maple syrup instead of the sugar bowl. Molasses is also a good substitute and also packs a nutritional punch, but has a much bolder, richer flavor (See **Kitchen Tip #52**).

126. Ever wondered what to do with the end of a box of cereal (besides throw it out) that no one wants to eat because there isn't enough to make a full bowl, or it's too crumbly or pulverized to eat? Or those mini boxes that come in the mail that would take 3 or 4 boxes in one sitting to satisfy the appetite? Add it to your stovetop oatmeal. This works great with those boxes of cereals that include raisins, blueberries, almonds, strawberries, etc., in them. Add the leftover cereal the same time you add the oatmeal and cook them both for the same amount of time, adding more water if needed, until desired consistency. This not only adds variety to the oatmeal and expands the meal, but it also helps sweeten it because of the sugar content in the boxed cereal. For additional sweeteners, use maple syrup to give your family a shot of vitamins and minerals at the same meal (See **Kitchen Tip #125**).

127. To prevent mineral deposits from forming in the bottom of the double boiler pan, add 1 teaspoon of vinegar to the water.

128. Use frozen waffle squares or the round version to make a quick sandwich. Toast waffles and spread with peanut butter and jelly or sandwich meats with your favorite condiments for a quick, easy sandwich. They also make great grilled cheese sandwiches and the kids won't ask you to cut off the crust.

129. Use tea bags to condition your hair. Brew 2–4 tea bags in 2 quarts of water. Let mixture cool, then remove

tea bags and pour mixture over your hair. Do not rinse. It gives hair a warm golden, shiny appearance and is especially great for dry, dyed, bleached, or coarse gray hair, and it rinses out beautifully on the next shampoo. It's the "wow" factor!

130. Besides for cooking, keep coconut oil on hand to control frizzy, curly hair. Rub a small amount into palm and smooth over and under curls. It gives hair a shiny, natural look and controls frizz, and is also good for dry scalp problems. Coconut oil is also a natural sunscreen. Used under SPF brands will help prevent the body's absorption of those chemicals when more protection from the sun is needed.

131. The next time you get a sore throat, try soothing it with a vinegar and honey remedy. Mix about ¼ cup of cider or white vinegar with about ¼ cup of honey and take 1 tablespoon six times a day. The vinegar and honey both kill bacteria.

132. Drop a marshmallow in the bottom of an ice cream cone before filling to stop the drip.

133. Use PAM, or no–brand cooking spray to quickly dry freshly painted finger and toenails. It works better and faster than most quick dry nail polish and great for women on the go!

134. Make your own natural eye wash with 1 tablespoon organic or pure apple cider vinegar, 2 tablespoons of organic or pure honey, mixed with 5 tablespoons of

pure filtered or distilled water. Add one drop to each eye daily with an eyedropper to relieve itchy, red eyes and to remove spots that aren't necessarily on your glasses. This is an astringent and will sting for a second or two, cause the eyes to water, which removes the debris that adheres to the outer layer of the eye causing those spots or blurred vision. This concoction was a favorite of my grandmother, Helen, and has no shelf life. You'll be amazed at how quickly it works and how much better you can see, truly.

135. Uniodized sea salt is a natural healer and should be in every household filled with active children or adults. Fill bathtub with warm water and pour a half container of salt in (along with bubbles if desired), and soak for 15–30 minutes. This salt bath speeds the healing process of superficial scrapes and cuts, and eases muscle tension and bruised areas. Used on a regular basis, it also aids in the removal of dried skin bumps, leaving skin smooth and soft on kids of all ages.

136. Pure organic cider vinegar can be used to speed up the healing of skin bruises and sunburns. Soak a cotton ball with vinegar and apply to bruised area or sunburned skin a few times daily. If many areas of the skin are sunburned, fill bathtub with cool or tepid (slightly warmed) water and add about a cup or two of the cider vinegar to the bath water and soak for about 15–20 minutes to take the major sting out of the burn. After the bath, immediately apply a

water–based, perfume–free lotion mixed with extra virgin olive oil (equal parts of each), or vitamin E oil to rehydrate the skin after the bath and throughout the day. Equal parts of pure coconut oil mixed with the extra virgin olive, or vitamin E oil may be used instead, as both naturally block sunrays. Cover up burned areas with white, cotton clothing if going back outdoors. The sun will penetrate through darker clothing, but not white. Note: If sunburn is severe and blistering or peeling, seek professional medical attention immediately.

137. Add extra virgin olive oil or coconut oil to your favorite moisturizer (or use by itself) before applying makeup. It helps moisturize dry skin, gives your facial skin extra protection from the sun, and it helps to evenly distribute your foundation. The best part is the olive or coconut oil absorbs quickly into the skin without looking greasy. And you thought these oils were used only for cooking!

138. Use distilled white vinegar to remove sweat stains on collars and under arm areas on clothing. Pour undiluted vinegar on stain, rub into stained area, let soak for 15–30 minutes and wash as usual. One or two cups in the wash with regular detergent and/or bleach will help brighten the entire load. It works great and your laundry won't smell like vinegar!

Kiss the Cook!

FOOD STORAGE TIPS:

139. To extend the shelf life of lettuce, celery, green peppers, an unused portion of onion, or fruits, and to keep them from getting rusty or slimy, rewrap them in dry paper towel sheets and refrigerate.

140. Buying your favorite cheese in blocks is the best bargain still. Grate as you like it and store the remaining cheese in frost–free or freezer bags or containers and freeze it. The cheese maintains it texture and flavor without the mold. Oil is a wonderful sealer for leftover tomato sauce, tomato paste, spaghetti sauce, salsa, and to preserve fresh herbs, etc. Just pour a layer of oil (whatever oil available is fine) on top of your leftover sauce or fresh herbs and refrigerate until you're ready to use it again. Pour the oil off before use. Paper towels can be used to absorb all the oil or put container in the freezer until the remaining oil has solidified somewhat to remove. This will keep the mold at bay and will preserve the sauce for a couple of weeks or longer, or preserve herbs for months.

141. Keep berries fresh longer by placing a paper towel over and under them in an airtight container. The paper towel collects the extra moisture, which keeps the berries from getting mushy or soft.

142. When freezing fresh blackberries, blueberries, or raspberries, never wash them first. Place a wet paper towel on a cookie sheet with sides and gently roll berries to remove debris and discard the bad ones. Remove paper towel, separate berries on cookie sheet with raised edges, and freeze overnight. Place frozen berries in freezer–proof bags and freeze until needed.

143. If you store cottage cheese upside down in its container in the refrigerator, it will keep twice as long.

144. Rinse unused pasta in a colander with water, let drain, drizzle a tablespoon or two of olive or cooking oil over it, toss to coat evenly, and store in the refrigerator for up to a week. This keeps the pasta from sticking together.

145. Store leftover packages of nuts (pecans, walnuts, peanuts, almonds, etc.) in your refrigerator to keep them as fresh tasting as the day you bought them. Set aside a crisper drawer for your nut and other baking items, including coconut and brown sugar, to keep them fresh until you use them again. Brown sugar will remain soft if kept stored in the refrigerator (See **Kitchen Tip #111**).

146. Store shortening, lard, or specialty oils (sesame, peanut, etc.) in the refrigerator to keep them tasting fresh after each use. Cold shortening or lard is also easier to remove from the measuring cups. Oils, lards, and shortenings develop a rancid, stale taste quicker

in warmer climates when stored in cupboards (See **Kitchen Tip #3**).

147. Store flour and rice products in the refrigerator or freezer during hot weather to extend the shelf life of these products. This will also stop the invasion of those annoying little white moths that hatch in these types of products. Nuts should also be stored in the refrigerator for this reason and to keep them from tasting stale or rancid.

148. Keep opened and unopened bags of potato or corn chips in the freezer to keep them fresh longer. The chips may be cold, but they retain their crispy texture and salty flavor, really!

149. Store leftover red or white wine in ice cube trays and freeze to use in future recipes. The wine freezes perfectly, and it's a great way to enhance the flavor of soups, sauces, stuffing, or any wild game, beef, chicken, fish, or pork dish.

150. Popcorn should always be kept in the freezer. It stays fresher longer and helps reduce the amount of un–popped kernels.

FOOD SIGNATURE FACTS

Maybe there is some truth to that old saying, "You are what you eat." This information about signature foods first came to me from a number of my email contacts, several times around actually. I finally traced one of the emails to the website of Don Tolman at www.dontolmaninternational.com. After doing a little research about Mr. Tolman and others sites relative to this subject, I knew I had to share the information about these foods with my family and friends. Another article that impressed me about the importance of these foods to our overall health and well being was written by Ingrid Cassel in a July 2008 issue of the Idaho Observer called, "God's handiwork: The Doctrine of Signatures". (http://proliberty.com/observer/20080704.htm) Ms. Cassel writes that these foods were referred to as the "doctrine of signatures" by past civilizations centuries ago, which alluded to a theory that each and every whole food resembles a physiological body function or body organ. The article goes on to say that modern food science today has proven that these foods do in fact have a positive effect on those organs that they resemble and that this information is referred to by today's modern scientists as the Teleological Nutritional Targeting, which contends, or states that every whole food's pattern resembles an organ or its function and acts as a 'sign' or 'signal' to the eater as to the foods' benefits. Wouldn't it be great to eat a few celery sticks every day instead of a pill to avoid bone fractures as we age? The following is just plain good information about foods that we should be eating daily and/or weekly. So for your good health, read on.

SIGNATURE FOODS:

Carrots: If you slice a carrot, it resembles the human eye, complete with pupil, iris, and radiating lines. And science has proven that carrots increase function and blood flow to the eyes.

Tomato: Tomatoes have four chambers and are red just like our heart. Science and research has shown that this food is actually food for our heart and blood.

Grapes: Grapes hang in clusters that resemble the heart, and each grape resembles a blood cell. Research has determined that grapes are indeed a heart and blood vitalizing food.

Walnuts: Walnuts resemble the brain, complete with a left and right hemisphere, upper cerebrum, lower cerebellum, and wrinkles or folds just like the neo–cortex. Science has proven that walnuts help develop over three dozen neuron transmitters for brain function.

Kidney Beans: Kidney beans are shaped just like our kidneys, and science has proven that they in fact help heal and maintain kidney function.

Celery, Bok Choy, Rhubarb, etc.: These foods resemble our bones, and in fact, specifically target bone strength. Our bones are 23 percent sodium, and these foods are 23 percent sodium. Without enough sodium in our diets, our bodies pull it from our bones, making them brittle. These foods replenish the sodium our skeletal system needs. The next time you break a bone, reach for the celery!

Avocadoes, Eggplant, & Pears: Avocadoes, eggplant, and pears resemble the cervix and womb, and research has shown that they target the health and function of these two organs. Research has also shown that if a woman eats one avocado a week, it balances her hormones, helps shed pregnancy birth weight, prevents cervical cancer, and more. And ironically, it takes exactly nine months for an avocado to grow from blossom to ripened fruit. Amazing!

Sweet Potatoes: Sweet potatoes resemble the pancreas and actually help balance the glycemic index of diabetics.

Truly amazing!

Olives: Research has proven that olives assist the health and the function of the ovaries.

Grapefruits, Oranges, Lemons, Limes & other citrus: When these fruits are cut in half, they resemble the female mammary glands. Research has proven that these citrus fruits actually assist the health of breasts and with the movement of the lymph in and out of the breasts.

Onions: Onions look like body cells, and research has shown that they clear waste materials from all of the body, including the eyes. The tearing we experience when we cut an onion is actually washing the epithelial layers of our eyes.

Figs: Research has shown that figs increase the movement and number of sperm in males. They also grow on the vine in twos and are full of seeds.

Bananas, Cucumbers, Zucchini, etc.: These fruits and vegetables are known to target the size and strength of the male sexual organ.

Peanuts: Research has proven that peanuts affect the testicles and sexual libido. Argentine, which is the main component of Viagra, comes from peanuts. Who knew?

Look for more like these in the next edition!

USING SPICES

The use of spices can greatly enhance the flavor of foods and turn an ordinary dish into an extraordinary one. Many spices have also been used for medicinal purposes over the centuries, and although I may have included this information with a particular spice, if you are pregnant or undergoing any medical treatment, please consult your physician prior to using a spice for this purpose.

Spices also have an expiration date and to test its freshness, please refer to **Kitchen Tip #114**. Fresh herbs can be preserved in oil, per **Kitchen Tip #140**, or used to make infused oils and complete instructions to do this can be found in the "Make Your Own" condiments section. They can also be stored in the freezer for up to a year and still maintain their fresh scent and flavor when heated if sealed in an air–tight frost–free container. Fresh dried herbs can be stored in recycled jars, and should be kept away from direct sunlight.

Most recipes call for the use of dried spices. To substitute fresh for dried, use 1 tablespoon of fresh chopped herbs per 1 teaspoon of the dried variety. To harvest fresh herbs, cut or snip as you need them and make the cut just above the next set of leaves. This manner of cutting will also stimulate the plant to grow taller and thicker.

To pay the least amount for dried spices and spiced salts, especially if you're not sure if it's one you'll like, shop for them at the local dollar stores.

SPICES

Allspice: Derived from an evergreen that grows up to forty feet tall. Its flavor is a blend of cinnamon, nutmeg, and cloves. It can be used in tomato sauces, with meats, gravies, fish, relishes, as well as desserts.

Anise: Derived from an evergreen tree that grows about ten to fifteen feet tall, this produces a star–like, brown fruit whose seeds taste like licorice. These dried seeds and oil are used in breads, rolls, cookies, and liqueurs. These crushed seeds added to a cup of warm milk will induce sleep.

Basil: This herb is a member of the mint family, and is the main ingredient in pesto sauces, besides the pine nuts and garlic. It has a sweet, clove–like flavor. It can be used fresh or dried in soups, salads, with meats or vegetables, and its pungency increases with cooking. Fresh leaves keep their flavor if preserved in oil or vinegar. Basil is a great herb that can enhance any meal, but tends to be expensive during winter months. It grows well and plentiful in any garden during warmer months, which is the best time to make and store your pesto sauce to save money.

Bay Leaves: Bay leaves are derived from the Bay tree and have a pungent, fragrant aroma. They enhance the flavor of tomato sauces and soups, and can be used in stews, with meatloaf, or vegetables. This spice is best used dried at the start of the cooking process, and should be removed before serving.

Celery Seeds: Derived from a plant similar to the celery plant we use as a vegetable. The plant produces tiny seed–like fruit that is tangy and has the fragrance of fresh celery. They are great in green salads, potato salads, pickles, stewed tomatoes, egg dishes, fish, cheese dishes, pot roasts, and most other vegetables.

Chervil: This herb has a delicate flavor, similar to tarragon, and can be used in place of parsley. It's great chopped fresh in salads, omelets, in salad dressings or with roasted chicken. Blend with cream cheese to stuff celery stalks as a snack or salad dish. When cooking this herb, add additional at the end as this herb does lose flavor during the cooking process.

Cinnamon: This spice is derived from a tropical evergreen tree that reaches twenty to thirty feet tall with thick, pale, smooth bark, and leathery green leaves that produce white flowers and bluish fruit. The dried inner bark is used as a spice in teas, coffee, cooked fruit, pickling liquids, honey, and mulled red wines. The ground inner bark is used in baking, puddings, and meat and fish dishes. Cinnamon adds a sweet taste to foods without the addition of sugar. Add one teaspoon of ground cinnamon to a bowl of oatmeal, along with a few chopped walnuts and test this theory for yourself. The ground seeds and seed oils are used in potpourris and perfumes. Cinnamon has been used medicinally for centuries to calm the stomach, pain in menopause, pain in the chest, back, and neck, and has been used to ease menstrual cramps or spasms and diarrhea. The Japanese discovered that cinnamon contains a substance that is both antifungal and antibacterial. This spice is not recommended for women who are pregnant.

Cloves: Derived from a tropical evergreen tree that reaches up to thirty feet tall, this spice produces a bell–shaped red flower. The unopened flower buds are dried and used to enhance the flavor of meats, especially hams, meat loafs, pork, spiced cakes, gingerbread, soups, mulled wines, and pickling. It can be used in pomanders, potpourri, infused as a tea to relieve nausea, and clove oil can be used to relieve tooth pain. It's this oil that a dentist uses to numb the gum before administering a shot of Novocain.

Coriander Seed: This herb is the ripe fruit of a small plant whose flavor resembles the combination of lemon peel and sage. This is a great seasoning for wild game stuffing, vegetables, soups, sauces, poultry dishes, and cookies. It's also known as cilantro or Chinese parsley in plant form and used to flavor Mexican and Chinese recipes.

Cumin: A delicate annual plant of the parsley family, it produces pinkish flowers followed by aromatic seeds. The seed from this plant has a distinctive salty, sweet flavor, and is the main flavoring ingredient in chili powders. This spice is used in American, Oriental, Indian, Mexican and Middle Eastern cooking to flavor meats, vegetables, cheeses, eggs, rice, fish, and chili. This spice packs a punch, so use sparingly. This spice is also known to be an appetite stimulator.

Curry Powder: This powder is a blend of spices including turmeric, a favorite of India and Middle Eastern cuisine, and is used to enhance rice dishes, flavor meats, poultry, fish, vegetables, sauces, and juices.

Dill: This plant is an annual of the parsley family and its tiny seeds can be used in pickling, to flavor salads, vegetables, cheeses, or soups. The tender, spicy greens of the plants can be used in salads, added as a garnish to cooked fish or steaks, flavor cream cheese, mayonnaise, butter, vegetables, soups, or pickling recipes.

Fennel: This spice is derived from a perennial plant of the parsley family. It has a mild licorice flavor and is similar in taste to the anise seed. The tender leaves or the swollen bulb of the plant can be chopped into salads, soups, vegetable medleys, or used to stuff fish or meats for additional flavor. The seeds can be used in potato salads, pickling, sauces, breads, or added to water for poaching fish. Fennel is great for the digestive system and reputed to be a dieting aid, as it curbs the appetite and alleviates hunger pains.

Garlic: This is a bulbous annual plant that belongs to the lily family. The edible root is made up of many small sections called cloves, and these have more flavor than the oil or powder versions. Rub a clove around the inside of a salad bowl to subtly flavor a tossed salad, or bake the entire bunch and serve with toast wedges and crackers as an appetizer. Garlic can be used to flavor meat, poultry, or fish dishes, flavor vegetable, soups, rice, and breads. Garlic is a natural antibiotic, assists in controlling fevers, is used as a topical treatment for warts, and works to combat viruses and harmful bacteria within the body.

Ginger: This tropical perennial plant grows three to four feet tall and produces an edible, buff colored, tubular root system that has a tangy, spicy flavor. Remove the buff colored skin, and the grated, fresh ginger can be used in teas, liqueurs, chutneys, fruits, Chinese dishes, breads, pies, cakes, poultry, meat or fish dishes, vegetables or soups. Powdered ginger has less flavor than the fresh variety. The fresh roots can be frozen. Fresh ginger tea or chewing on fresh ginger will soothe a sore throat, and instantly warm the body. This method will also settle an upset stomach and ease motion sickness while traveling.

Mace or Nutmeg: This tree is in the evergreen family, grows to about twenty–five feet tall, and produces a fruit after its flowering period. The outer covering, or aril, of the seed of this fruit is called mace. Nutmeg is the actual seed of the fruit. Both of these spices are similar in taste to each other. Mace has a milder, nutty flavor like that of cinnamon and can be substituted as needed. Nutmeg has a more intense flavor and can make a recipe taste bitter if overused. A little goes along way with nutmeg. Use in breads, pies, cakes, cookies, vegetables, meats, stews, soups, milks, cordials, liqueurs, poultry, lamb, beef, fruits, and sauces. This spice has been used to stimulate the appetite and aid in the digestion process.

Marjoram: This herb is from the mint family and has a pungent evergreen smell and taste. Use sparingly or to taste on meats, stews, soups, sauces, vegetable, salads, dressings, cheese, and egg dishes, or stuffing. Marjoram can be used in place of sage or oregano if necessary (see oregano and sage).

Mustard: This spice is derived from the seeds of the mustard plant. These seeds are small and spicy hot and are used in pickling mixtures, with vegetables, soups or stews, etc. The ground mustard is used in potato salads, pot roasts, spreads, and dips.

Nutmeg: See mace.

Oregano: This herb is from the mint family and is similar in flavor to marjoram, only slightly more pungent. Use sparingly or to taste on meats, stews, soups, sauces, vegetable, salads, dressings, cheese and egg dishes, or stuffing. Marjoram can be used in place of sage or oregano if necessary (see marjoram and sage).

Paprika: A mild member of the pepper family, this spice adds mainly color with a trace of flavor to meats, fish, deviled eggs, sauces, vegetable, and salads, but no spicy heat.

Parsley: A green herb with a mild, distinctive flavor used in beverages, salads, soups, sauces, stews, and omelets, to flavor meat, poultry, vegetable, or fish dishes. The stems have a more intense flavor. It's also great as a garnish and can be used as a breath freshener after a meal. This herb is loaded with vitamins and minerals so make sure to swallow it after chewing.

Rosemary: Derived from a small evergreen shrub and looks like a pine needle, this herb has a somewhat bitter taste and adds a "bite" to foods. It can be used in sauces, salads, stuffing, with vegetables, meats, foul, fish, eggs, breads, biscuits, fruit salads, teas, etc. After the needles have been removed, the stalks can be soaked in water and used as skewers for shish kabobs on the grill to add additional flavor to your meat or vegetables. Rosemary is reputed to be an antioxidant herb and a strong brain and memory stimulant. Rosemary tea has been used to treat mouth sores, calm the nerves, and aids in the digestion of fat. This herb should be in everyone's garden.

Saffron: This herb is from the inner portion of a flower in the crocus family called the stigma. The stigma receives the pollen within the flower and it takes 225,000 of them to make a pound, which is why it's the world's most expensive spice. Its unique flavor is unusual, and a little goes a long way. It has a pungent, strong aroma and only a pinch is needed to flavor or add a yellow to orange color to a recipe. If used in baking, this herb should be crushed and added to the liquid in the recipe first, then blended with the solids for best results. Used in rice recipes, cookies, cakes, breads, fancy rolls or biscuits, poultry, meats, seafood, soups, sauces, etc. Saffron can promote perspiration, which helps the body eliminate toxins through the skin, and has been used for its anti–inflammatory abilities in the treatment of gout, arthritis, and bursitis.

Sage: This annual herb grows to about three feet tall, has long, gray leaves that have a strong distinctive flavor and fragrance. The flowers are collected and used for teas. The leaves can be used fresh or dried in soups, stews, stuffing, with fish, meats, vegetable, fruits, tomatoes, breads, muffins, biscuits, rice, cheeses, or butter spreads, infused with vinegar, used to flavor appetizers, etc. This herb has many medicinal qualities and was thought to be the herbal savior of mankind in ancient times. It's been used to control night sweats during menopause. It's also been used as an underarm deodorant, and has been reputed and used to dry up breast milk when nursing mothers begin to wean their young. It also aids in the digestion of fats, is credited for being a powerful antioxidant, and so much more. This herb should be in everyone's garden. If the leaves have a musky aroma, discard and chop or grind the stems, which also contain the fragrant oils and benefits of this herb. Pregnant women or nursing mothers should avoid this herb. Oregano or Marjoram are similar in taste and can be substituted.

Tarragon: This perennial herb grows to about eighteen inches tall, and has a mild, sweet flavor. It's great in sauces, and the main herb in Hollandaise and béarnaise sauce, perfect in soups, stews, butter, or cheese spreads, meat, poultry, or fish dishes, stuffing, tartar sauce, vinegar, salads, eggs, in appetizers, or marinades. It's the best in homemade chicken soup and a favorite in my kitchen. It can be expensive to buy, but grows great in any garden or herb bed; it is also a perennial, which means it re–seeds itself and comes back every year.

Thyme: This herb is a member of the mint family and has a strong, fresh, aromatic scent and flavor. The dried variety of this herb is less potent and pungent than the fresh variety, and fresh thyme should be used sparingly so as not to overwhelm a recipe. There are a few varieties of this herb, including French, English, lime, and lemon thyme. It can be used to flavor sauces, stews, meats, poultry, fish, soups, salads, appetizers, etc. This herb has been around for centuries and is widely used in medicine as an antiseptic, as well as a germicide. The oil of this herb is used in gargles, toothpaste, and mouthwashes, including Listerine. Thyme leaves can be used as a warm poultice to treat skin eruptions and fungal infections and in tea form to treat respiratory and digestive system ailments. This herb has no restrictions on its use and is another that should be in everyone's garden for good health.

Turmeric: This spice is derived from the orange colored root of a plant in the ginger family and is an important ingredient in curry powder. It has a mild, slightly bitter flavor, and should be used sparingly in a recipe, especially in baking. The ground form can be used in curries, mustards, pickling mixtures, in meat or fish dishes, eggs, etc. It can be used whole or ground form, and can be substituted for Saffron in a recipe for coloring cakes, cookies, breads, rice, icing, etc., creating a yellow colored product.

RECIPES OR NOTES

ABBREVIATIONS

T=tablespoon

t=teaspoon

oz=ounce

fl. oz=fluid oz

lb=pound

C=cup

pt=pint

qt=quart

gal=gallon

pk=peck

bu=bushel

in=inch

ml=milliliter

l=liter

g=grams

cc=cubic centimeter

cm=centimeter

kilo=kilogram

in=inch

ft=foot

yd=yard

ea=per each

approx.=approximately

RECIPES OR NOTES

FOOD EQUIVALENTS

1 pound brown sugar	= 2¼ cups packed
1 pound granulated sugar	= 2¼ cups
1 pound confectioners' sugar	= 3½ cups
1 medium lemon (room temperature)	= 3–4 tablespoons juice & 1 tablespoon grated peel (zest)
½ pint whipping cream	= 1 cup un-whipped or 2 cups whipped cream
6 ounces chocolate chips	= 1 cup
4 ounces cheese	= 1 cup shredded
1 cup broth	= 1 teaspoon instant or 1 cube plus 1 cup water
1 pound of butter	= 2 cups
1 cup butter milk	= 1 tablespoon of vinegar or lemon juice+ 1 cup whole milk
1 ounce of chocolate (unsweetened)	= 3 tablespoons cocoa plus 1 tablespoon fat (shortening, etc.)
1 tablespoon instant onion	= ¼ cup chopped onion

List continues to next page

½ teaspoon powder onion	= 1 tablespoon chopped onion
1 cup cake flour	= 1 cup minus 2 tablespoons all purpose flour
1 cup all purpose flour	= 1 cup plus 2 tablespoons cake flour
1 tablespoon flour	= ½ tablespoon cornstarch
1 cup honey	= ¾ cup sugar plus ¼ cup liquid (water, juice, etc.)
1 cup molasses	= ½ cup sugar + ¼ cup liquid (water, juice, etc.)
1 cup heavy cream	= 1/3 cup butter plus ¾ cup milk
1 cup raw rice	= 3½ cups cooked
1 cup dry beans (legumes)	= 2½ cup cooked
1 pound fresh cranberries	= 3–3 1/3 cups sauce
15 graham crackers	= 1 cup fine crumbs
5 ounces peanuts	= 1 cup
4½ ounces chop pecans	= 1 cup
3¾ ounces pecan halves	= 1 cup
4½ ounces chop walnuts	= 1 cup
3½ ounces walnut halves	= 1 cup
½ pound macaroni/spaghetti noodles	= 4 cups cooked noodles

List continues to next page

1 pound of tomatoes	= 3 medium tomatoes
12 chocolate sandwich cookies	= 1 cup crumbs
20 chocolate wafers	= 1 cup crumbs
24 vanilla wafers	= 1 cup crumbs
8 large marshmallows	= 1 cup miniature marshmallows
1 cup chocolate chips (6 ounces)	= 4 squares chocolate (1 ounce)
1 pound flour	= 3½–4 cups
1 stick butter or margarine	= 8 tablespoons or ½ cup
¼ cup fresh milk	= 1 tablespoon dry milk

U.S. MEASUREMENT CONVERSIONS

1 gallon (gal) = 4 quarts = 8 pints = 16 cups = 128 fluid ounces
1 quart (qt) = 2 pints = 4 cups = 32 fluid ounces
1 pint (pt) = 2 cups = 16 fluid ounces
½ pint (pt) = 1 cup = 8 fluid ounces
1 cup = 8 fluid ounces = 16 tablespoons = 48 teaspoons (tsp)
¾ cup = 12 tablespoons = 36 teaspoons
2/3 cup = 10 tablespoons + 2 teaspoons
½ cup = 8 tablespoons = 24 teaspoons = 4 ounces
3/8 cup = 6 tablespoons = 18 teaspoons
5/8 cup = ½ cup + 2 tablespoons = 10 tablespoons
7/8 cup = ¾ cup + 2 tablespoons = 14 tablespoons
½ of 1/3 = 2 tablespoons + 2 teaspoons
1/3 cup = 5 tablespoons + 1 teaspoon = 16 teaspoons
¼ cup = 4 tablespoons = 12 teaspoons = 2 ounces
1/6 cup = 2 tablespoons + 2 teaspoons = 8 teaspoons
1/8 cup = 2 tablespoons = 6 teaspoons
1/16 cup = 1 tablespoon = 3 teaspoons
1 tablespoon = ½ fluid ounce
1 tablespoon = 3 teaspoon
1/3 teaspoon = a heaping ¼ teaspoon
2/3 teaspoon = a heaping ½ teaspoon
1 1/3 tablespoon =1 tablespoon + 1 teaspoon
½ tablespoon = 1½ teaspoon
Dash or pinch = 1/16 teaspoon or half of 1/8 teaspoon (also called a "speck")

List continues to next page

16 ounces = 1 pound	
8 ounces = ½ pound	
4 ounces = ¼ pound	
2 ounces = 1/8 pound	
4 pecks = 1 bushel	
8 quarts = 1 peck	

U.S. TO METRIC MEASUREMENT CONVERSIONS

U.S.	METRIC
MEASUREMENT (DRY)	
1/8 teaspoon (tsp)	0.5 ml (milliliter)
¼ tsp	1 (ml)
¾ tsp	4 ml
1 tsp	5 ml
1 T	15 ml
¼ cup	60 ml
1/3 cup	75 ml
½ cup	125 ml
2/3 cup	150 ml
¾ cup	175 ml
1 cup	250 ml
2 cups	1 pint = 500 ml
3 cups	750 ml
4 cups	1 quart = 1 liter
4 quarts	1 gal. = 3.8 liters

MEASUREMENT (LIQUID OR FLUID)	
1 fluid ounce	2 T = 30 ml
4 fluid ounces	½ cup = 125 ml
8 fluid ounces	1 cup = 250 ml
12 fluid ounces	1½ cups = 375 ml
16 fluid ounces	2 cups = 500 ml
34 fluid ounces	1 liter

List continues to next page

WEIGHT (SOLID)	
.035 oz	1 gram
½ oz	15 grams
1 oz	30 grams
3 oz	90 grams
3.5 oz	100 grams
4 oz	120 grams
8 oz	225 grams
10 oz	285 grams
12 oz	360 grams
16 oz	450 grams
1.10 lb	500 grams
35 oz	2.205 lbs = 1 kilogram
1 lb	16 oz = 450 grams
1 inch (in)	2.54 centimeters (cm)
1 milliliter (ml)	1 cubic centimeter (cc)

BAKING PAN SIZES: U.S. TO METRIC

DISH/PAN	SIZE (INCHES/ QUARTS)	METRIC VOL.	CENTIMETERS
Square	8x8x2	2 Liters	20x20x5
Square	9x9x2	2.5 Liters	22x22x5
Rectangular	12x8x2	3 Liters	30x20x5
Rectangular	13x9x2	3.5 Liters	33x23x5
Loaf pan	8x4x3	1.5 Liters	20x10x7
Loaf pan	9x5x3	2 Liters	23x13x7
Round cake pan (single)	8x1-1/2	1.2 Liters	20x4
Round cake pan (single)	9x1-1/2	1.5 Liters	23x4
Pie plate	8x1-1/4	750 milliliters	20x3
Pie plate	9x1-1/4	1 Liter	23x3
Casserole	1 quart	1Liter	--------
Casserole	1-1/2 quart	1.5 Liter	--------
Casserole	2 quart	2 Liter	--------

U.S. TO METRIC DIMENSIONS

1/16 inch = 2 millimeters
1/8 inch = 3 millimeters
¼ inch = 6 millimeters
½ inch = 1.5 millimeters
¾ inch = 2 centimeters
1 inch = 2.5 centimeters

OVEN TEMPERATURES:
250 degrees = 120 degrees Celsius
275 degrees = 140 degrees Celsius
300 degrees = 150 degrees Celsius
325 degrees = 160 degrees Celsius
350 degrees = 180 degrees Celsius
375 degrees = 190 degrees Celsius
400 degrees = 200 degrees Celsius
425 degrees = 220 degrees Celsius
450 degrees = 230 degrees Celsius

CONVERTING BETWEEN THE METRIC & U.S. SYSTEM

IF YOU KNOW:	MULTIPLY BY:	TO FIND:
WEIGHT		
Grams	0.035	Ounces
Kilograms	2.2	Pounds
Ounces	28	Grams
Pounds	0.45	Kilograms
LENGTH		
Millimeters	0.04	Inches
Centimeters	0.4	Inches
Meters	3.3	Feet
Kilometers	0.6	Miles
Inches	2.54	Centimeters
Feet	30	Centimeters
Yards	0.9	Meters
Miles	1.6	Kilometers

List continues to next page

VOLUME		
Milliliters	0.2	Teaspoons
Milliliters	0.07	Tablespoons
Milliliters	0.03	Fluid Ounces
Liters	4.23	Cups
Liters	2.1	Pints
Liters	1.06	Quarts
Liters	0.26	Gallons
Teaspoons	5	Milliliters
Tablespoons	15	Milliliters
Fluid Ounces	30	Milliliters
Cups	0.24	Liters
Pints	0.47	Liters
Quarts	0.95	Liters
Gallons	3.8	Liters

RECIPES OR NOTES

_____

_____

_____

_____

_____

_____

_____

_____

_____

_____

_____

_____

_____

_____

_____

MY PERSONAL WEIGHT MANAGEMENT GUIDE

IT'S ALL ABOUT THE NUMBER

I was once totally convinced that losing weight was truly the hardest thing for any human to do, and this human was no exception. I've tried just about everything, from grapefruit to vinegar, cabbage soup, dealing a meal, proper food combining, protein only, the Thigh Master, even incorporating aerobic exercise and Pilates classes to lose weight over the past couple of decades.

I was always looking for the quickest and the easiest way to lose a few pounds, searching for that one magic process or pill that would rapidly melt away the pounds to reveal the Marilyn Monroe figure I knew was there somewhere. And I did lose weight using some of these methods, especially the exercise classes. However, I knew some were only a temporary fix on my long-term weight loss endeavor. I also knew that after a few weeks back to my old eating habits, I'd be looking for a new diet method to help me lose the weight that I just gained, that I just lost, that I just gained. And everything was working out just fine until I quit smoking.

I'd been a cigarette smoker for twenty-eight years and vowed that when the price per pack went to five dollars, I was going to quit. They did, and I kept my word. The patches and hypnotism cured my addiction. And for the first twelve months, I took my doctor's advice and focused on breaking the cigarette habit and not on the weight gain. It was more like thirty-six months before I finally took a look at just how much weight I'd really gained. And it was much more than a temporary fix could handle this time. I had gained nearly forty pounds. I definitely needed a structured plan.

I knew Weight Watcher's had been around forever, helping people lose weight, and I also knew that their program could get pricey with the visits and the foods, so I went the cheaper route. I borrowed the food point system guidelines from someone that had participated in their program and bought the Weight Watcher's Cookbook at my local bookstore to save a buck. I planned my meals according to the point system, and did lose a few pounds as long as I stuck with the point value menu items.

What I found difficult about this particular plan was that I would inevitably eat something that didn't have a point value assigned to it along with those that did, which ultimately ended with me not counting any points at all. I did learn to make healthier meals with this program, but the weight still wasn't coming off as fast as I thought it should, and this point counting stuff was too limiting for me. I wanted a weight loss program that I could realistically incorporate in my daily life for the rest of my life without worrying about points. I thought there had to be a better program. A friend suggested I check out the LA Weight Loss program. I took her advice.

Not only did I check them out; I joined their weight loss program in January of 2003. They immediately structured my meals, gave me a menu, and told me what foods, what snacks, what beverages, and what time to consume them. There was nothing to calculate. They count the calories for you. You eat specifically what is on the menu repeatedly in conjunction with exercise for the duration of time you need to lose the desired weight. It worked and it works. I lost weight, but soon got bored eating the same thing every week. It also was too expensive for me to maintain forever. I just needed to lose a little weight, not my life savings in the process.

When I compared the LA Weight Loss plan and the Weight Watcher's plan, I noted another similarity about each besides the obvious weight loss factor. I noticed that both programs count the calories for you in their own unique way. They each assign their own unique numbers to the food and beverage meals associated with their plans. This makes it pretty hard for anyone to maintain the weight loss from their programs unless one continues with their programs. I figured that calories must be pretty important if both of these groups either omit the actual caloric value of foods and beverages or have created a whole new numbering plan around them. This made me take a closer look at these calories and their correlation to my weight.

So exactly what is a calorie? One dictionary's definition says it's the unit of measurement of energy produced by food when used, or oxidized, in the body. If a calorie is energy and I'm taking in more caloric energy than I really need, which then propels the extra caloric energy towards my hips, thighs, and stomach, then this was a concept I could finally understand. And, this measurement is expressed in a numerical form. It can therefore be said that a calorie is just a number. Obviously a very important number, but a number just the same.

And what is a number? A number is a fixed value for every single function on this planet, including the function of weight control. And if one human pound is equivalent to thirty-five hundred (3,500) caloric units of energy, that meant that I was still carrying around about 70,000-plus units of unnecessary power somewhere around my middle and backside that had to go.

At least now I had real numbers associated with this problem—numbers that I could put into my own math equation and realistically manage my weight for the long run without looking to the next fad diet or using expensive assistance, coupled with expensive, premade foods to help me lose the excess pounds. If one pound is equal to 3,500 calories, and I reduced the caloric energy of food I eat daily by five hundred, and do this every day for seven days, as 7 x 500 = 3,500, then I could lose a pound a week. If I didn't change what I ate, only used exercise to burn five hundred calories a day for seven days, I'd lose a pound a week. If I worked the two together, I could potentially lose more than a pound, but at least a pound a week. Could it really be that simple?

Armed with this new knowledge, I began to put my own weight-loss program in place. I first created my own quick reference chart of the true caloric values for foods and beverages I consumed daily, weekly, or whenever. This gave me the ability to keep track of the total number of calories I was taking in daily. I wrote down the caloric number for every single thing that passed my lips every day, whether it was food, a beverage, or a condiment, for seven days. It was a tedious task, but I needed to know my number—the actual number of calories I was eating daily. I then added those seven daily totals together and divided by seven. This gave me a single number, which was the average number of caloric energy, or calories, that I intake or eat daily without even thinking about it.

It's this number that I used in my own personal weight-loss equation. I then subtracted five hundred from that number, which gave me my new daily caloric energy number that would assure me a one-pound loss in one week. I used the quick reference chart to plan my own variety of meals around this new number, meals that appealed to me individually. I also traded foods with lower caloric numbers and ate more of them to feel full. I just kept track of the real numbers associated with these foods. It's all about the numbers. When I plateau and can't seem to get past a certain weight, I repeat the process of documenting every-

If you have health issues, please consult your physician before attempting any weight loss program.

thing I eat or drink again for a week, subtract five hundred from that new number to continue my pound a week weight loss until I reach a weight I'm comfortable with.

It's not a miracle plan, pill, or potion, and nor is it a quick fix. And it's a tedious task to write down everything that goes into your mouth daily, but a necessary one. It's also a task that doesn't need to be repeated very often unless you can't seem to get past a certain weight.

This method has turned out to be the long-term weight management plan I was looking for, as well as an inexpensive alternative to all the other weight loss programs I've either tried or researched.

Calories are obviously essential to weight management, and the extensive list I've compiled of the caloric numbers associated with various foods I've consumed, even the fast food variety, has made it easier for me to keep track of them and control my weight. Having all the information in one point of reference makes remembering the caloric number of a particular food item easy. It helps me to make better food choices while staying within my caloric energy range without feeling like I'm on a diet. I still buy fast food every now and again; I just limit the amount I eat and keep track of the caloric number associated with it.

A seven-day task of self-monitoring your caloric energy intake and a simple math equation is the key to individual weight control. Once you are armed with this knowledge about you, it will be hard not to lose weight or gain it, should that be the case. At the very least, you'll understand why the scale never moves, or goes in the wrong direction to your liking. Weight management is all about the numbers.

RECIPES OR NOTES

_____

_____

_____

_____

_____

_____

_____

_____

_____

_____

_____

_____

_____

_____

_____

_____

HOW TO CALCULATE YOUR WEIGHT CONTROL NUMBER

SUNDAY:
Total calorie intake for the day = 2,495

MONDAY:
Total calorie intake for the day = 2,050

TUESDAY:
Total calorie intake for the day = 1,907

WEDNESDAY:
Total calorie intake for the day = 2,140

THURSDAY:
Total calorie intake for the day = 1,890

FRIDAY:
Total calorie intake for the day = 2,325

SATURDAY:
Total calorie intake for the day = 2,500

TOTAL CALORIES FOR THE WEEK: = 15,307

15,307 divided by seven (7) days = 2,187 calories per day

3,500 calories = 1 pound of body weight.

7(days) x 500 calories = 3,500 calories = 1–lb (pound) gain or loss.

2,187–500 (per day) = 1,687 (per day) = My new weight control number to lose one pound a week.

This 2,187 number is the average amount of calories I consume each day without a conscious thought. Since 3,500 calories is equal to one human pound, if I subtract or reduce 500 calories a day from my 2,187 number, my new weight control number is 1,687.

If I do not allow myself to exceed 1,687 calories a day for seven days (500 calories x 7 days = 3,500), I'll lose a pound a week, guaranteed. If I incorporate a little stretching or exercise in that week to burn additional calories, I can potentially lose more weight to reach a goal I'm comfortable with. And I can create my own menu around the foods I like because I now know the real caloric energy number associated with them. How simple is that? And it really works!

In addition to metric conversions, as well as some other useful information, I've included a guide for appropriate weight goals for men and women and a chart of calories burned during specific exercises. These figures are just a guide, as everyone is an individual and carries weight differently, so five or ten pounds over or under this figure may be your perfect weight. If you incorporate exercise into your daily routine, you may burn more or less calories depending on your starting weight. The more you weigh, the more calories you'll burn during exercise. And the reverse is also true.

My best advice is to not kill yourself with exercise. Swimming and stretching exercises are my preference. These cause the least amount of stress and damage to bones and joints while toning muscles and burning calories. You don't have to exercise to lose weight using this method, but it does help to tone and firm the excess skin that results from the weight loss.

Just be patient and persistent. If it took three years to gain the weight, be prepared to take three years to remove it. It's better for your health and body to do so in the long run. Just keep track and memorize the caloric numbers of the foods that pass your lips daily.

Weight control is all about these numbers.

RECIPES OR NOTES

WEIGHT CHARTS FOR
MEN AND WOMEN

WOMEN (AGES 25-59)

HEIGHT	SM. FRAME/LBS.	MED. FRAME/LBS.	LG. FRAME/LBS.
4'10	102–111	109–121	118–131
4'11	103–113	111–123	120–134
5'0	104–115	113–126	122–137
5'1	106–115	115–129	125–140
5'2	108–121	118–132	128–143
5'3	111–124	121–135	131–147
5'4	114–127	124–138	134–151
5'5	117–130	127–141	137–155
5'6	120–133	130–144	140–159
5'7	123–136	133–147	143–163
5'8	126–139	136–150	146–167
5'9	129–142	139–153	149–170
5'10	132–145	142–156	152–173
5'11	135–148	145–159	155–176
6'0	136–151	148–162	158–179

List continues to next page

MEN (AGES 25-59)

HEIGHT	SM. FRAME/LBS.	MED. FRAME/LBS.	LG. FRAME/LBS.
5'2	128–134	131–141	138–150
5'3	130–136	133–143	140–153
5'4	132–138	135–145	142–156
5'5	134–140	137–148	144–160
5'6	136–142	139–151	146–164
5'7	138–145	142–154	149–168
5'8	140–148	145–157	152–172
5'9	142–151	148–160	155–176
5'10	144–154	151–163	158–180
5'11	146–157	154–166	161–184
6'0	149–160	157–170	164–188
6'1	152–164	160–174	169–192
6'2	155–168	164–178	172–197
6'3	158–172	167–182	176–202
6'4	162–176	171–187	181–207

*Information obtained from www.heathchecksystems.com, www.dietbites.com, www.trulyhuge.com

CALORIES BURNED DURING EXERCISE OR PHYSICAL ACTIVITIES

ACTIVITY	CALORIES BURNED PER HOUR
Walking, 2 mph	240
Walking, 3 mph	320
Walking, 4.5 mph	440
Jogging, 5.5 mph	740
Jogging, 7 mph	920
Jumping Rope	750
Swimming, 25 yards/min.	275
Swimming, 50 yards/min.	500
Running in place	650
Running, 10 mph	1,280
Bicycling, 6 mph	240
Bicycling, 12 mph	410
Cross Country skiing	700
Tennis-singles	400
Horseback Riding	288

List continues to next page

ACTIVITY	CALORIES BURNED PER 10 MINUTES
1. Aerobics (high intensity)	100
2. Gardening	49
3. Racquetball	90
4. Shopping	42
5. Sleeping	12
6. Volleyball	34
7. Walking upstairs	175
8. Sitting (reading or watching TV)	12

*NOTE: The above figures are approximate and based on a person weighing 150 pounds. The more you weigh, the more calories you'll burn. If you weigh less than 150 pounds, these figures will decrease.

*Information obtained from www.peublo.gsa.gov, dated 02/09/2006

CALORIC ENERGY NUMBERS

FOODS	
MEATS	**CALORIES**
Beef Tenderloin (3.5 oz.)	255
Bologna spread (2 oz.)	277
Chicken (dark meat/skinless, 3 oz.)	178
Chicken (skinless, 3.5oz)	167
Club Steak (3½ oz.)	190
Cornish Hen (6 oz.)	372
Duck (6 oz.)	916
Filet Mignon (9 oz.)	360
Goose (6 oz.)	329
Ground Lamb (3 oz.)	241
Ground Turkey (3.5 oz.)	233
Ground Veal (3.5 oz.)	144
Ham (lean, boiled, 3 oz.)	200
Hamburger (lean, broiled, 3 oz.)	185
Italian Sausage (1 link)	268
Lamb (lean grilled, 4 oz.)	200
Lamb Leg Roast (3 oz.)	235
Liver (3½ oz.)	210
Loin Roast (3½ oz.)	340
Moose (3.5 oz.)	134
New York Strip (12 oz.)	630
Ostrich (3 oz.)	97

List continues to next page

Pate De Foie Gras (1 oz.)	130
Pheasant (3 oz.)	82
Polish Sausage (1 hot dog link)	145
Pork Chop (3 oz., med.)	340
Pork Roast (3 oz.)	310
Pork Sausage (3 oz.)	405
Porterhouse Steak (3½ oz.)	290
Pot Roast (round cut, 3½ oz.)	200
Prime Rib (16 oz.)	1,280
Quail (1 whole, meat only)	120
Quail (1 whole, with skin)	210
Rib Eye (13 oz.)	610
Rib Lamb Chop (3 oz., med.)	300
Rib Roast (3½ oz.)	260
Rump Roast (3½ oz.)	340
Salmon Spread (1 oz.)	219
Sirloin (12 oz.)	410
Swiss Steak (3½ oz.)	300
T Bone (16 oz.)	800
Turkey breast (6 oz.)	266
Veal Chop (3 oz., med.)	185
Veal Roast (3 oz.)	230
Venison (deer loin, 3.5oz.)	150
FISH AND SEAFOOD	
Anchovies (5, in olive oil)	42
Blue Crab (3 oz.)	87
Bluefish (3 oz.)	105
Carp (3 oz.)	138

List continues to next page

Catfish (3 oz., fried)	195
Caviar (1 tablespoon, red/black)	40
Clams (20 small, fried)	380
Crabmeat (4 oz., canned, drained)	70
Crayfish (3 oz., steamed)	97
Flounder (3 oz.)	99
Grouper (3 oz.)	100
Haddock (3 oz.)	95
Halibut (3 oz.)	119
Herring (0.5 oz., pickled)	39
Herring (1.5 oz., Kippered)	87
Herring (3 oz.)	173
King Crab (3 oz.)	82
Lobster (3 oz.)	83
Mackerel (3 oz., Atlantic)	223
Mackerel (3 oz., King)	89
Mahi-mahi (3 oz.)	72
Monkfish (3 oz.)	65
Mullet (3 oz.)	128
Mussels (3oz., blue)	146
Octopus (3 oz.)	70
Orange Roughy (3 oz.)	107
Oysters (6 medium, fried)	173
Oysters (6 medium, steamed, raw)	60
Perch (3 oz., Ocean)	103
Pike (3 oz.)	96
Pollack (3 oz.)	96
Pompano (3 oz.)	179

List continues to next page

Roe (3 oz., fish)	119
Salmon (3 oz., Chinook)	99
Salmon (3 oz., smoked)	100
Salmon (3.5 oz., Atlantic)	206
Salmon (4 oz., canned)	200
Sardines (1 oz. in oil)	50
Scallops (2 large, steamed)	67
Scallops (4 oz., 12 small, bay)	100
Sea Bass (3 oz.)	42
Shark (3 oz., fresh)	130
Shrimp (3 oz.)	80
Shrimp (3 oz., fried)	206
Shrimp (3 oz., steamed)	84
Smelt (3 oz.)	105
Snapper (3oz., Red)	109
Snow Crab (3oz., cooked)	95
Sole (3 oz., Dover)	99
Squid/Calamari (3 oz., fried)	149
Striped Bass (3 oz.)	82
Sturgeon (3 oz., smoked)	147
Sword (3 oz.)	132
Tilapia (3 oz., fresh)	110
Trout (3 oz., Rainbow)	128
Tuna (1/4 cup, canned, drained)	60
Tuna (3 oz., fresh)	111
Whitefish (3 oz.)	92

*The FDA recommends that fish such as shark, swordfish, king mackerel, and tilefish not be eaten by expectant mothers as they contain high levels of a form of mercury called methyl mercury that may harm the fetus's developing nervous system.

List continues to next page

VEGETABLES	
Acorn Squash (1 cup mashed)	83
Asparagus (8 oz., canned)	35
Asparagus (8 oz., fresh)	35
Baked Beans (8 oz.)	320
Butternut Squash (1 cup mashed)	80
Beets (1 cup, canned)	80
Beets (3.5 oz., pickled)	65
Beets (3/4 cup, fresh)	44
Broccoli (1 cup)	52
Carrots (1 cup, raw, chopped)	52
Cauliflower (1 cup, fresh)	25
Celery (1 cup, diced)	17
Chick Peas (1 cup canned)	260
Collard greens (1 cup, cooked)	27
Collard Greens (1 cup, raw)	11
Corn (1 cup, canned)	170
Corn (1 cup, creamed, canned)	200
Corn (1 cup, fresh, cooked)	180
Corn (1 ear, fresh)	59
Cucumber	13
Eggplant (1 cup, raw)	20
Green Beans (8oz., fresh)	30
Green onion (1/4 cup, chopped)	10
Leeks (1/2 cup, raw)	27
Lettuce (1 cup, shredded)	6
Lima Beans (8 oz., fresh)	180
Mushroom (1 cup, raw)	16

List continues to next page

Mustard greens (1 cup, cooked)	15
Onions (1 cup, raw)	61
Parsnips (1 cup, raw)	100
Peas (1 cup, canned)	165
Peas (1 cup, fresh)	115
Potatoes (2½ in. diameter, baked)	100
Potatoes (2½ in. diameter, boiled)	100
Potatoes(1 cup, mashed)	240
Radishes (1 cup, pickled)	33
Radishes (1 cup, sliced)	23
Rutabaga (1cup, cubed)	51
Sauerkraut (1 cup)	27
Spinach (1 cup, fresh)	40
Succotash (1 cup, fresh)	260
Summer Squash (1 cup, fresh)	30
Tomato Paste (2 tablespoons)	30
Tomato Sauce (1 cup, canned)	80
Tomatoes (1 cup, canned)	100
Turnip greens (1cup, cooked)	20
Turnips (1 cup, cubed)	35
Turnips, Green (1 cup, raw)	18
Water Chestnuts (1 cup)	90
Winter Squash (1 cup, fresh)	130

*Food Fact: Succotash is a vegetable dish consisting mainly of lima beans and corn.

List continues to next page

FRESH FRUIT	
Apples (1 medium)	52
Apricot (3.5 oz.)	28
Apricots (3.5 oz.)	28
Avocado (1 oz., medium)	55
Banana (1 whole)	133
Blueberries (3.5 oz.)	56
Boysenberry (8 oz.)	66
Cantaloupe (3.5 oz.)	32
Cherries (3.5 oz.)	53
Crabapple (1.7 oz.)	45
Dates (fresh, seeded, 1.75 oz.)	54
Figs (1 oz.)	63
Gooseberries (3.5 oz.)	19
Grapefruit (3.5 oz.)	27
Grapes (dark, 3.5 oz.)	63
Grapes (green, 3.5 oz.)	56
Guava (3.5 oz.)	60
Honey Dew Melon (5.4 oz.)	50
Kiwi Fruit (3 oz.)	36
Lemon (1 small)	20
Lime (1 small)	17
Lime (1, peeled)	9
Mango (4 oz.)	86
Nectarine (3 oz.)	30
Orange (4 oz.)	44
Peaches (4 oz.)	44
Pear (6.5 oz.)	74

List continues to next page

Pineapple (4 oz.)	42
Plum (3.5 oz.)	36
Pomegranate (3.5 oz.)	51
Prunes (stewed, no sugar, 3.5 oz.)	78
Raspberry (3 oz.)	16
Rhubarb (3.5 oz.)	7
Strawberry (3.5 oz.)	27
Watermelon (3.5 oz.)	23
BEVERAGES	
2% Low-fat Milk (8 oz.)	120
7-Eleven Cola (32 oz. Big Gulp)	300
Buttermilk (8 oz.)	99
Club Soda, low salt (8 oz.)	0
Coffee (1 cup, black, 8 oz.)	9
Cola (12 oz.)	140
Cola (8 oz.)	100
Decaf Coffee (1 cup, black, 8 oz.)	0
Dunkin Donut Coffee Coolatta (16 oz.)	350
Dunkin Donut Coffee Coolatta with skim milk (16 oz.)	170
Gatorade (20 oz.)	150
Gingerale/7-Up (8 oz.)	100
Half & Half Cream (1 tablespoon)	20
Heavy Cream (1 tablespoon)	52
Light Coffee Cream (1 tablespoon)	30
Light Hawaiian Punch (12 oz.)	10
Milk (1 cup, chocolate)	257
Nantucket Nectars Lemonade (16 oz.)	180

List continues to next page

Ohana Lemonade (8 oz.)	90
Seltzers, Diet Sodas, & Fruit2O's	0
Skim Milk (8 oz.)	90
Soy Milk (8oz.)	90
Sparkling Water	0
Starbucks Iced Caramel Macchiato (16 oz.)	270
Tea (1 cup, 8 oz., no sugar)	2
Tonic Water (8 oz.)	90
Whipping Cream (1 tablespoon)	44
Whole Milk (8 oz.)	150
ALCOHOL 80-PROOF DISTILLED SPIRITS	
Brandy/Whiskey (1 oz.)	64
Gin (1 oz.)	64
Guinness Stout Beer (12 oz.)	126
Light Beer (12 oz.)	108
Red Wine (5 oz.)	105
Regular Beer (12 oz.)	144
Rum (1 oz.)	64
Sweet Dessert Wine (3 oz.)	141
Tequila (1.5 oz., 80-proof)	97
Vodka (1 oz.)	64
White Wine (5 oz.)	100
DAIRY FOODS	
Butter (1 tablespoon)	100
Cheese (1 oz. Parmesan, grated)	55
Cheese (1 oz., Brick)	104
Cheese (1 oz., Caraway)	95
Cheese (1 oz., Edam)	100

List continues to next page

Cheese (1 oz., Fondue)	62
Cheese (1 oz., Goat Cheese)	76
Cheese (1 oz., Gouda)	100
Cheese (1 oz., Mozzarella)	72
Cheese (1 oz., Pepper Jack)	110
Cheese (1 oz., Provolone, cubed)	58
Cheese (1 oz., Ricotta)	43
Cheese (1 oz., Romano)	110
Cheese (1 oz., Swiss)	95
Cheese (1 tablespoon, Parmesan, shredded)	21
Cheese (1oz., American)	105
Cheese (1oz., Blue cheese)	99
Cheese (1oz., Cheddar)	113
Cheese (1oz., Cheshire)	108
Cheese (1oz., Colby)	110
Cheese (1oz., Feta)	74
Cheese (1oz., Fontina)	109
Cheese (1oz., Gruyere)	116
Cheese (1oz., Muenster, diced)	61
Cottage Cheese (½ cup)	110
Cream Cheese (1 oz.)	98
Egg (1 large, white only)	17
Egg (1 large, yolk)	59
Eggs (1 large)	76
Margarine (1 tablespoon)	100
Sour Cream (1 tablespoon)	31
Yogurt (1 cup, whole milk)	139

*Egg Fact: In addition to being a good source of A and B vitamins, iron and riboflavin, the egg yolk has been used by artists for centuries in many of their tempera paints.

List continues to next page

CONDIMENTS	
A-1 Sauce (1 tablespoon)	15
Grape Jelly (1 tablespoon)	50
Honey (1 tablespoon)	64
Ketchup (1 tablespoon)	15
Maple Syrup (organic, 1 tablespoon)	53
Mayonnaise (1 tablespoon)	100
Miracle Whip (1 tablespoon)	40
Molasses (1 tablespoon)	60
Mustard (1 teaspoon, Dijon)	0
Mustard (1 teaspoon, yellow)	0
Olive Oil (1 tablespoon)	120
Salsa (1 tablespoon)	5
Soy Sauce (1 tablespoon)	11
Strawberry Jelly (1 tablespoon)	50
Sweet relish (1 tablespoon)	20
Tabasco Sauce (1 teaspoon)	0
Vegetable Oil (1 tablespoon)	120
Vinegar (flavored) (1 Tablespoon)	10
Vinegar (white or cider)	0
Worcestershire Sauce (1 teaspoon)	0
BREADS	
Bagel (2 oz.)	160
Bread Pudding (1 cup)	475
Buttermilk (1 slice)	80
Cornbread (1.5 oz.)	95
Croissant (1 small)	117
English Muffin (2 oz.)	150
Foccacia (1 oz.)	125

List continues to next page

French (1.25 oz.)	100
Hamburger Bun (1 plain)	170
Hot Dog Bun (1)	160
Italian (1 slice)	83
Multigrain Wheat (1 slice)	70
Pumpernickel (1 slice)	80
Raisin (1 slice)	65
Rye (1 slice)	60
Sourdough (1 slice)	70
Wheat (1 slice)	65
White (1 slice)	70
PASTAS & RICE	
Angel Hair (4 oz., uncooked)	372
Cannelloni (4 oz., uncooked)	325
Gnocchi (4 oz., uncooked)	340
Jasmine rice (1/4 cup, uncooked)	180
Light Egg Noodles (1¼ cup, uncooked)	210
Long Grain (Uncle Ben's, 1 cup, cooked)	170
Long grain white rice (3/4 cup, cooked)	160
Macaroni, elbow (½ cup, uncooked)	210
Minute rice (½ cup, cooked)	200
Orzo (1/4 cup, uncooked)	210
Spaghetti (4 oz., uncooked)	338
Spaghetti, Wheat (4 oz., uncooked)	305
Spinach Linguine (1½ cup, uncooked)	210
Vermicelli (4 oz., uncooked)	338

List continues to next page

NUTS & BAKING CONDIMENTS	
Almonds (¼ cup, whole)	170
Brown Sugar (1 teaspoon)	15
Butterscotch Morsel bits (1 tablespoon)	70
Cocoa (1 tablespoon)	20
Chocolate Morsel Bits (1 tablespoon)	80
Cornmeal (3 tablespoons)	110
Cornstarch (1 tablespoon)	30
Lard (1 tablespoon)	116
Maple syrup (1 tablespoon)	53
Oatmeal (½ cup)	150
Pecans (¼ cup, whole)	210
Pine Nuts (1/4 cup)	170
Pistachio (1 oz.)	165
Powdered Sugar (¼ cup)	120
Shortening (1 tablespoon)	100
Walnuts (¼ cup)	200
White Sugar (1 teaspoon)	15
White Flour (¼ cup)	100
FAST FOOD	
McDonald's Bacon, Egg, Cheese McGriddle	450
McDonald's Baked Apple Pie	250
McDonald's Big & Tasty	470
McDonald's Big Breakfast	730
McDonald's Big Mac	560
McDonald's Biscuit	240
McDonald's Cheeseburger	310
McDonald's Chicken Fajita	190

List continues to next page

McDonald's Chicken Nuggets (10)	420
McDonald's Chicken Nuggets (20)	840
McDonald's Chicken Nuggets (6)	250
McDonald's Chicken Snack Wrap	323
McDonald's Child 12 oz. Coke	110
McDonald's Cinnamon Roll	340
McDonald's Coke, Large	310
McDonald's Double Cheeseburger	460
McDonald's Double Quarter Pounder	770
McDonald's Egg McMuffin	300
McDonald's Egg McMuffin, no meat	280
McDonald's Filet of Fish	380
McDonald's Fish Filet Deluxe	560
McDonald's Fries (large)	570
McDonald's Fries (medium)	380
McDonald's Fries (small)	250
McDonald's Fruit & Walnut Salad	310
McDonald's Grilled Chicken Club	590
McDonald's Grilled Chicken Flatbread	340
McDonald's Hamburger	280
McDonald's Hotcakes (no syrup)	340
McDonald's Hotcakes Syrup & Margarine	560
McDonald's Hot-n-Spicy Chicken Sandwich	450
McDonald's Kiddie Cone	45
McDonald's Low-Fat Apple Bran Muffin	300
McDonald's McChicken	430
McDonald's McChicken, no mayo	300
McDonald's McChicken, spicy, no mayo	330

List continues to next page

McDonald's McRib Sandwich	490
McDonald's McValue Fries	320
McDonald's McVeggie Burger with Wheat	360
McDonald's Orange Juice (12 oz.)	140
McDonald's Oreo McFlurry	560
McDonald's Quarter Pounder	410
McDonald's Quarter Pounder with Cheese	510
McDonald's Sausage Biscuit	410
McDonald's Sausage Burrito	300
McDonald's Sausage McMuffin	370
McDonald's Steak, Egg, Cheese Bagel	640
McDonald's Super-Size Fries	610
McDonald's Triple Chocolate Shake (16 oz.)	580
Burger King Bacon Double Cheeseburger	638
Burger King Bacon Double Cheeseburger Deluxe	708
Burger King Cheeseburger	367
Burger King Chicken Nuggets (4 pieces)	220
Burger King Chicken Nuggets (7 pieces)	385
Burger King Double Whopper with Cheese	1060
Burger King Dutch Apple Pie	308
Burger King Hamburger	325
Burger King Large Fries	450
Burger King Orange Juice (Large)	231
Burger King Regular Onion Rings	330
Burger King Veggie Burger	685
Burger King Whopper	670
Burger King Whopper (no meat)	405

List continues to next page

Hardee's Monster Burger	1420
Del Taco 1-pound beef burrito	1170
Taco Bell Bacon Cheeseburger Burrito	560
Taco Bell Big Beef Burrito Supreme	520
Taco Bell Big Beef Nachos Supreme	430
Taco Bell Breakfast Quesadilla with Bacon	460
Taco Bell Breakfast Quesadilla with Sausage	440
Taco Bell Burrito Supreme	440
Taco Bell Chicken Club Burrito	540
Taco Bell Chicken Fajita Wrap Supreme	500
Taco Bell Chili Cheese Burrito	330
Taco Bell Cinnamon Twists	140
Taco Bell Double Bacon & Egg Burrito	480
Taco Bell Double Decker Taco	340
Taco Bell Gordita Fiesta, Grilled Chicken	280
Taco Bell Gordita Fiesta, Grilled Steak	270
Taco Bell Kid's Soft Taco Roll-up	290
Taco Bell Light Chicken Burrito	310
Taco Bell Light Chicken Burrito Supreme	430
Taco Bell Light Chicken Soft Taco	180
Taco Bell Mexican Pizza	570
Taco Bell Mexican Rice	190
Taco Bell Nachos	310
Taco Bell Nachos Bell Grande	740
Taco Bell Pintos & Cheese	190
Taco Bell Regular Taco	170
Taco Bell Seven Layer Burrito	540
Taco Bell Soft BLT Taco	340

List continues to next page

Taco Bell Soft Taco	210
Taco Bell Steak Fajita Wrap Supreme	510
Taco Bell Steak Soft Taco	200
Taco Bell Taco Salad (no shell)	420
Taco Bell Taco Salad (shell only)	270
Taco Bell Taco Supreme	220
Taco Bell Tostada	300
Taco Bell Veggie Fajita Wrap Supreme	460
Big Boy 2 oz. Tartar Sauce	370
Big Boy Brawny Lad Sandwich	420
Big Boy Buddie Boy	760
Big Boy Chili (regular serving)	315
Big Boy Fish Sandwich	690
Big Boy Onion Rings	580
Big Boy Regular Big Boy	600
Big Boy Regular Fries	360
Big Boy Slim Jim Sandwich	325
Big Boy Small Hamburger	445
Big Boy Super Big Boy	830
Big Boy Swiss Miss Sandwich	635
Wendy's 10 oz. Baked Potato, plain	270
Wendy's 12 oz. Chili	330
Wendy's 14 oz. Baked Potato, Bacon & Cheese	440
Wendy's 14 oz. Baked Potato, Broccoli & Cheese	330
Wendy's 2.5 oz. Fries	208
Wendy's 4 oz. Chocolate Frosty	161
Wendy's 5 oz. Caesar Salad with everything	270
Wendy's Big Bacon Classic	590

List continues to next page

Wendy's Chicken Club	650
Wendy's Chicken Nuggets, 4 pieces	190
Wendy's Child Cheeseburger, 4.3 oz.	320
Wendy's Child Ham & Cheese Sandwich, 4.2 oz.	240
Wendy's Child Hamburger, 4.3 oz.	270
Wendy's Child Turkey & Cheese, 4.5 oz.	250
Wendy's Classic Single with cheese	420
Wendy's Classic Single, no cheese	370
Wendy's Classic Triple with cheese	970
Wendy's Crispy Chicken	380
Wendy's Crispy Chicken Deluxe	450
Wendy's Fish Sandwich	480
Wendy's Frescata Club	440
Wendy's Frescata Turkey & Basil	420
Wendy's Frescata Turkey & Cheese, no mayo	250
Wendy's Half Pound Bacon Cheddar Double	770
Wendy's Junior Double Cheese Deluxe	460
Arby's Apple Turnover with icing	377
Arby's Apple/Cherry Turnovers, no icing	247
Arby's Arby Melt, 5.1 oz.	302
Arby's Baked Potato Deluxe, 12.7 oz.	645
Arby's Baked Potato with butter & sour cream, 11.3 oz.	495
Arby's Baked Potato with Broccoli & Cheese	535
Arby's Baked Potato with Sour Cream, 10.8 oz.	393
Arby's BBQ Bacon & Jack Sandwich, 6 oz.	360
Arby's Beef & Cheddar, 6.9 oz.	445
Arby's BLT Wrap, 8.8 oz.	648

List continues to next page

Arby's Cheddar Fries, 6 oz.	465
Arby's Cherry Turnover with icing	377
Arby's Chicken Cordon Bleu, 8.6 oz.	650
Arby's Chipotle Grilled Chicken, 9.3 oz.	517
Arby's Crispy Chicken Filet, 8.4 oz.	576
Arby's Curly Fries, 7 oz.	631
Arby's Fish Sandwich, 8.1 oz.	569
Arby's French Dip Sandwich with Swiss	473
Arby's French Dip Sandwich, 7 oz.	391
Arby's French Dip Sub, 9.9 oz.	448
Arby's French Dip with Au Jus. 9.9 oz.	448
Arby's Fresh BLT Sandwich, 10.4 oz.	779
Arby's Fresh Corned Beef Sandwich, 10.9 oz.	606
Arby's Fresh Turkey Reuben, 10.9 oz.	611
Arby's Fresh Wrap Chicken with Pecans, 9.8 oz.	638
Arby's Fresh Wrap Corned Beef, 9.9 oz.	577
Arby's Grilled Chicken Filet, 8.2 oz.	414
Arby's Ham & Swiss Junior Melt, 3.5 oz.	211
Arby's Ham & Swiss Melt, 4.9 oz.	275
Arby's Home-style Fries, 7.5 oz	566
Arby's Hot Ham & Cheese, 5.9 oz.	304
Arby's Italian Sub, 9.8 oz.	622
Arby's Jalapeno Bites, 10 pieces	611
Arby's Kid's Fruit Cup, 2 oz.	35
Arby's Large Roast Beef Sandwich, 9.9 oz.	547
Arby's Loaded Potato Bites, 10 pieces	707
Arby's Mini Ham & Cheese	228
Arby's Mini Turkey & Cheese, 4 oz.	235

List continues to next page

Arby's Mozzarella Sticks, 4 pieces	426
Arby's Onion Petals, 10 oz.	828
Arby's Philly Beef & Swiss, 10.8 oz.	670
Arby's Potato Cakes, 1.8 oz.	123
Arby's Roast Beef Gyro, 8.5 oz.	542
Arby's Roast Beef Junior	272
Arby's Roast Beef Sub, 10.6 oz.	723
Arby's Roast Beef, 5.4 oz.	320
Arby's Roast Beef, 7.4 oz.	415
Arby's Roast Turkey Wrap with Ranch & Bacon	700
Arby's Sourdough Roast Beef Melt, 5.9 oz.	355
Arby's Southwest Chicken Wrap, 8.9 oz.	567
Arby's Swiss Melt, 5.1 oz.	303
Arby's Turkey Reuben Wrap, 9.9 oz.	581

*Fast food and select foods caloric value information obtained from www.thecalorieking.com, www.thedailyplate.com, www.dietbites.com, www.nutritionfacts.com, http://caloriecount.about.com, and food packaging of items consumed.

** Eating foods with the proper daily requirement of vitamins and minerals is essential to weight management. Consuming fresh fruits and raw vegetables daily will help meet these requirements.

EPILOGUE

I've come realize that all accomplishments start with a dream or a goal. The next step is to create a plan to make it a reality in whatever time frame is needed to do so. Life is full of obstacles that may slow you down for a moment of two. But the most important aspect of your focus is to maintain tunnel vision to keep your eye on the end result of all your efforts. Those efforts are essential to accomplishing your dream or goal.

The wisdom and knowledge gained along your journey will not only be personally rewarding, it is wisdom and knowledge gained that belongs to only you. It's also information that will serve you well in the future, and God willing, you'll be blessed to share your wisdom and knowledge with others to better assist them in their time of need.

My dream has been to show others who are on a tight budget how to save money in the most expensive room in a home—the kitchen. I'm proud to say I've partially accomplished my mission to do just that in this first edition of *The Kitchen Assistant*. However, there is so much more that I would like to share and look forward to doing so in future editions.

Sincerely,

Darla

RECIPES OR NOTES

INDEX

RECIPES OR NOTES